Macramé

By the Editors of Sunset Books
and Sunset Magazine

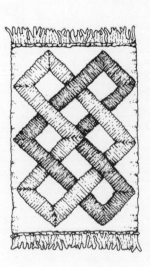

Lane Publishing Co. • Menlo Park, California

Acknowledgments

We would like to thank the following individuals for their suggestions and advice regarding the contents of this book: Helene Bress, Helen Freeman, Barbara Jee, Dona Meilach, Gertrude Reagan, and Ginger Summit.

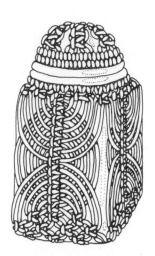

Edited by
Alyson Smith Gonsalves

Design: Tonya Carpenter

Illustrations: Nancy Lawton

Cover: Nubby Textured Rug (page 56) designed by Ginger Summit, and Sculptural Plant Hanger (page 59) designed by Joy Coshigano of Hidden House. Photo by Norman A. Plate.

Editor, Sunset Books: David E. Clark

Eighth Printing September 1979

Contents

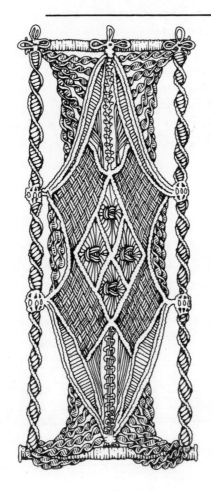

Loose macramé netting *from ancient Egypt, courtesy Museum of Fine Arts, Boston.*

Introducing Macramé

Macramé (pronounced mak′ra•mā) comes either from a 19th century Arabic term, *miqramah,* which meant veil, or from the Turkish word for towel, *maqramah.* Both the veil and the towel were adorned with a knotted fringe.

The handcraft known as macramé probably developed when man first needed to attach two lengths of cord or to bind two objects together in a permanent or semi-permanent manner. The square and hitch knots may date back to Paleolithic or Neolithic man, who undoubtedly used these knots in his daily life.

As time passed, knots were used for a variety of utilitarian, mnemonic, and superstitious purposes. However, once the beauty of the knots themselves was recognized, a new art form emerged.

History Repeats Itself

Existing examples of knotting date back to early Egyptian culture, when knots were used in fishnets and in decorative fringes (see facing page). The Incas of Peru used a *quipu,* a length of knotted rope constructed of mnemonic knots, to aid them in keeping mathematical records and other important information. In classical Greece, knots were used in medicine (as slings for broken bones) and in games (the Gordian knot was one such puzzle). Both the early Egyptians and Greeks used the Hercules knot (square knot), which had magical or religious connotations, on their clothing, jewelry, and pottery.

Knotting techniques were probably spread far and wide by sailors who, in their spare time, would create a multitude of knotted items to decorate their ships, to trade, or to give as gifts. The sailors on ancient sailing ships sometimes carried a knotted cord which, claimed legend, witches had tied. The knotted cord supposedly bound the winds and therefore controlled the destiny of the sailing ship.

Macramé in the sailors' vocabulary was better known as "McNamara's Lace" or "square knotting" because the square knot predominated in their work.

Evidence of macramé reaching North America can be seen in the work of the Northern California Indians after contact with Europeans. In the Victorian era, the

Want something special in the way of techniques? This chapter has them. Learn how to make a good start and a photo-perfect finish to your work. We've also added notes on shaping macrame, adding and subtracting extra cords, and special working techniques to give you some of that "edge" the experts possess.

stylish gowns and cloaks of the gentry in European society were adorned with macramé knots. Some craftsmen of that period, having even greater ambitions, created larger pieces, such as whole tablecloths, bedspreads, piano drapes, and even doorway curtains.

Today, macramé is enjoying a 20th century renaissance. As people find that they have more spare time, men as well as women are turning to such handwork, creating pieces that are both utilitarian and esthetic.

Great pleasure can be derived from evolving a seemingly intricate textile design through the use of only two basic macramé knots: the half hitch and the square knot. Since the combinations and variations of these two knots seem to be endless, they lend themselves to a vast array of two-and three-dimensional designs. And macramé is an individualistic craft—each person's style of knotting adds a unique touch to his work.

Macramé the Easy Way

A craft for all ages and capabilities, macramé is really an international concept found just about anywhere today from the United States to the People's Republic of China. Equipment and materials are available everywhere; all that's needed are cords or yarns for the knots themselves, a few pins, and a working surface large enough to accommodate the project you're creating. Most macramé can be carried with you and comfortably worked on any time.

Macramé projects have few limitations. For an idea of some of the possibilities open to you, take a look at the projects offered in this book, starting on page 34.

If you're a beginner, start out with the knotting instructions beginning on page 10. Then look over the section on color, texture, and design on page 30 for information on planning your work to avoid mistakes and to achieve maximum results.

Have you had previous experience with macramé? Then check out the section on general techniques (page 24) and the gallery of advanced work (starting on page 74) or go directly to the projects. You're sure to find something of interest.

Equipment You'll Need

Minimal equipment is needed for macramé—just a support for the work, pins to hold the work in place, and a few accessories to measure, cut, and bundle the working cord ends. Dime stores, craft shops, and lumber supply yards carry just about everything you'll need. Macramé equipment can be divided into three categories: working surfaces, pins, and miscellaneous materials.

Choosing Working Surfaces

The type of working surface you'll need will depend to a great extent on the size of your project, the materials you'll use, and the amount of working space you have available. Some surfaces are made specifically for macramé work; others can be temporarily adapted to your needs from furnishings already in your home.

Specifically for macramé

Fiber board and foam rubber slabs—light-weight and portable, with firm surfaces easily adaptable to most macramé work—are inexpensive and can be purchased in almost any size. Felt can be stapled to the fiberboard or pinned to the foam rubber to create an improved working surface (see facing page). Foam rubber comes in a number of shapes; the most useful and most easily located are flat slabs, pillow fillers, or bolster rolls.

Many Victorian macramé pieces were worked on heavy, sand-filled cushions, an idea that can be put to use today. Sew a pillow liner of heavy muslin, stuff it firmly with dry sand, and whip the edge shut; then cover it with a snugly fitting "sleeve" of felt.

The lap board (shown on facing page) is an easily made clamp and board frame for small macramé projects, such as belts and jewelry. Cut an 18-inch-long 1-by-4 board into 12-inch and 6-inch sections. With screws, attach paper clamps at one end of each board, in the center. Then join the two board lengths with a pair of offset hinges as shown in the photograph on the facing page. This frame can be folded flat for storage.

Some adaptations

Picture frames, purchased wooden or metal hoops, even a dress form or wig stand can serve for special macramé projects. Use the frames and hoops when you want your macramé to have a built-in

setting. Try the dress form or wig stand for such macramé pieces as hats, necklaces, or even entire garments that need to be shaped to fit.

Other adaptations can include ladder-back chairs, clipboards, or padded ironing boards. A mounting cord can be tied between the knobs of the chair; small pieces can be mounted on the clip board for a portable working surface or pinned down on the ironing board surface for working at home.

Pins for Macramé

You use pins to secure a macramé project to a working surface and to hold the shape of the piece while it is worked on. Use pins, too, wherever an area needs reinforcing or securing. A selection of pins suitable for macramé work is shown on the facing page. Push pins, card pins, and T-pins are available in stationery stores. Look for hat pins, plastic-headed sewing pins (only for small projects), or upholstery pins in sewing centers.

Miscellaneous Materials

You'll need some basic tools for measuring, cutting, and bundling cord lengths. Keep a scissors, tape measure, and yardstick on hand, as well as rubber bands, twist-ties, and plastic or cardboard bobbins (see page 35 for bobbin making). Use paper clamps to hold cords out of the way while you work. To measure off cord lengths, use a pair of C-clamps set at a distance equal to the length needed and attached upside down on a table edge.

For planning out your work ahead of time, make use of the varied graph papers sold in stationery stores. You can lay out the project design in terms of color and overall pattern, averting the chance of making mistakes later on.

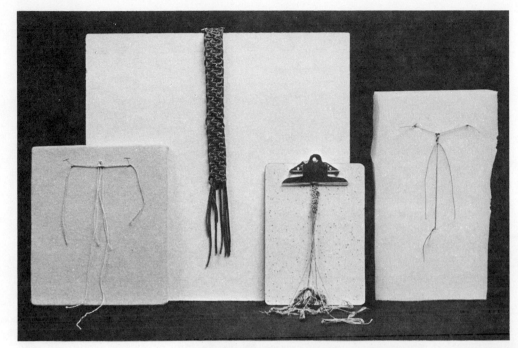

Conventional working surfaces *are shown here (left to right): felt-covered fiberboard, plain fiberboard, a clipboard, a thick foam slab.*

Unusual macramé supports *include (top to bottom): the stretcher bar frame, wig stand, homemade lap board.*

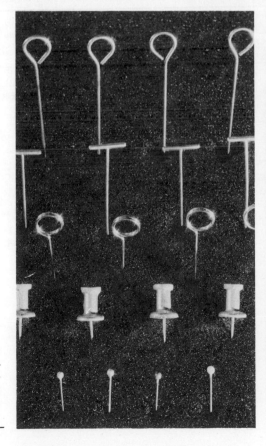

A selection of pins *for macramé (top to bottom): upholstery pins, T-pins, card pins, push pins, glass-headed pins.*

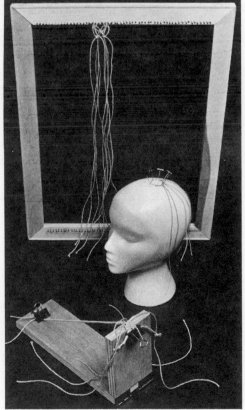

Materials for Macramé

Any pliable materials available in great lengths are suitable for macramé work. These can be comprised of anything from kite string or sisal rope to surgical tubing or fine wire. Some very unusual materials have been used for macramé; they include bed sheet strips, leather thong, paper twine, and rolls of plastic grocery bags.

The only absolute requirements are pliability and strength without undue stretchiness, suitability for the ultimate use to which a project will be put, and a surface quality that will enhance the design and the individual macramé knots. Knotting materials can be divided into three categories: vegetable fibers, synthetic fibers, and animal fibers.

Vegetable Fibers

The most popular of all macramé materials, vegetable fibers include jute, linen, and cotton. All are readily available, knot easily, come in a variety of weights and colors, and can be dyed. Most of these cords can be purchased in their natural finish, as well as with protective coatings like wax, creosote, or sizing.

Cotton. Found in many forms, cotton can be soft or stiff and comes in varied sizes, textures, and finishes. It is exceptionally strong and long-wearing. Naval and clothesline rope, as well as package string and perle cotton, fall into this category.

Jute. A brightly colored, prickly surface characterizes jute cord. But this material doesn't wear well; it can fade or rot, unless chemically treated, and it sheds during knotting.

Linen. Strong, smooth-surfaced, and lint-free—linen cord has these qualities. More expensive than most materials, linen nevertheless gives good knot definition and a soft, smooth overall texture.

Synthetic Fibers

Chemically produced fibers such as acrylic, polyester, nylon, rayon, and plastic metallics are considered synthetics. They are often combined with natural fibers, such as cotton or wool, to give added elasticity.

Acrylic and polyester. Soft, weather resistant, and warm, these two materials are excellent for use in clothing or projects for outdoor use. They dye well and usually come in bright colors.

Nylon and rayon. Available in silky, shiny braid or cord, these materials are beautiful but not easy to work with. Both tend to unravel and slip during knotting.

Metallic cord. This has a pliable rayon core wrapped with a thin strip of gold or silver-colored, plastic-coated metal. Metallic cord is used for clothing detailing and for jewelry work.

Animal Fibers

Wool, silk, and hair fibers are contributions from the animal kingdom. Of all types of yarns, these have the greatest color range; however, they have a tendency to stretch and break under tension, as well as to shed during knotting.

Wool. Soft, lightweight, and warm, wool comes in two different forms: wool worsted, a smooth strong yarn; and woolen, which has a fuzzy, soft appearance. Of the two, worsted is better suited to the pulling and stretching that occur during knotting.

Silk. A beautiful, strong yarn, silk is somewhat expensive for large macramé projects. It has a soft, slippery surface in its most common form and a rough texture when spun from tussah, or wild silk.

Hair. Taken from horses, goats, dogs, and other animals, spun hair has a prickly, coarse texture suitable for sculptural work or rugs.

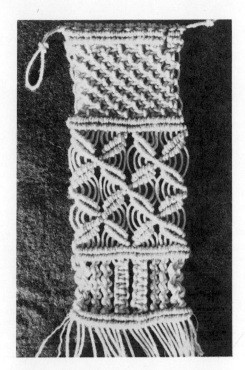

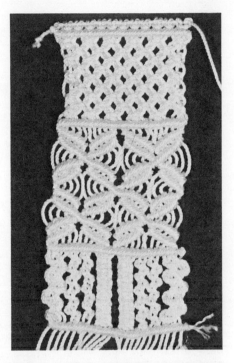

Linen produces a beautiful surface effect when knotted; it is soft and supple yet well defined. An elegant material to work with, linen is relatively expensive, and its color range is limited.

Jute is a colorful vegetable fiber that works up into a fuzzy, prickly-textured surface. In spite of a tendency to shed and fade, jute enjoys great popularity.

Nylon cord has a silklike surface quality and a beautiful appearance when knotted, though it's slippery to work with and tends to unravel unless the ends are sealed with glue or melted.

Wool enjoys a tremendous color range **(right).** It is the most versatile of knotting materials but not necessarily the strongest. A tendency to stretch and break under tension limits its use in macramé projects that must support weight.

Cotton cord **(left)** comes in a variety of sizes, textures, and colors. A strong, durable material, cotton cord produces well-defined macramé knots.

Basic Macramé Knots

It's a pleasant surprise to find that most macramé patterns, though complicated in appearance, generally employ only two knots: the square knot and the double half hitch. You can work out an endless number of variations by using multiples or combinations of these two knots tied in different directions or at different angles.

To add occasional decorative elements to these variations, combine them with Josephine and Turk's-head knots, wrapping, plaiting, or picots.

Taking the Mystery Out of Macramé

When taken as a whole, a macramé piece can appear as an undecipherable maze of knots and cord ends. This is not the least bit encouraging to the beginner; it can even be intimidating—but it doesn't have to happen to you.

First, learn the knots on the following 13 pages. Then you'll be able to zero in on specific areas of any macramé work by asking yourself these questions: "How was it started? What groups of knots do I recognize, and how were they combined? Is there a repeat or an overall plan to the pattern? How was this piece finished?" Memorizing the knots is the key to breaking the code.

Two approaches

You'll find there are two ways to master the basic macramé knots: 1) Explore each knot individually (this is the simplest method) or 2) Make a knotting sampler by working all of the knots with the same cords. The yarn and cord samplers on page 9 were formed in a similar manner. Making a sampler will help you to understand how knots interrelate with one another and also to compare the differences between knotted areas made with square knots and those made with double half hitches.

If you plan to work with each knot individually, cut as many 1-yard lengths of cord as the individual knotting directions call for; also cut a 10-inch length of cord to use as a mounting cord.

But if the idea of making a sampler appeals to you, different preparations are in order. Cut 12 cords, each 288 inches long, as well as a 20-inch length to use as a mounting cord. Fold the long cords in half and mount them at their midpoints

onto the mounting cord (see the instructions for mounting knots on the facing page).

Since long cord ends tend to tangle easily, it's best to wrap each end into a bobbin after your working cords have been mounted. Instructions for wrapping bobbins may be found on page 35.

Before you begin the sampler, pin the mounting cord to the working surface by tying an overhand knot at each end and pinning through each knot. From this point on, work all knots in their proper order from page 11. Picot headings are the only exceptions: there won't be room on the sampler for all the variations. Choose those you'd like to learn first for your sampler; then cut shorter lengths of cord to practice the remaining picots individually.

Using the Instructions

Instructions and their accompanying illustrations have been kept as simple as possible in order to avoid confusion. The knots themselves have been arranged in the order in which they are normally used: mounting knots first, followed by the double half hitch and the square knot, as well as by a number of their basic variations. Decorative techniques and knots (including picots) come last.

Use cord, rather than yarn, for learning the knots; it remains strong in spite of the great amount of friction, stretching, and tension it undergoes. The smooth surface qualities of most cords are ideal for macramé because they form clean-lined, well-defined knots.

Knots can be tied from left to right or vice versa. If you want to reverse the directions given, simply hold a small pocket mirror at a 90° angle to the illustrations to see the image backward.

Mounting Knots and Overhand Knot

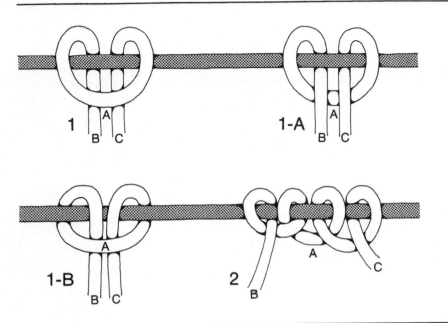

Mounting knots are used to secure working cords onto a support at the starting point of a piece or at an area where cords are being added. The two knots shown at left are those most often used.

1. Fold the working cord in half and place loop A under the mounting cord; then bring A down in front of the mounting cord (1). Pull ends B and C down through loop A (1-A). Pull knot tight. To reverse this mounting knot, work from front to back (1-B).

2. To form the double half hitch mounting knot, mount the cords as shown in 1-A. Then bring each end over and behind the mounting cord and out through the loops formed (2). Pull the cords tight.

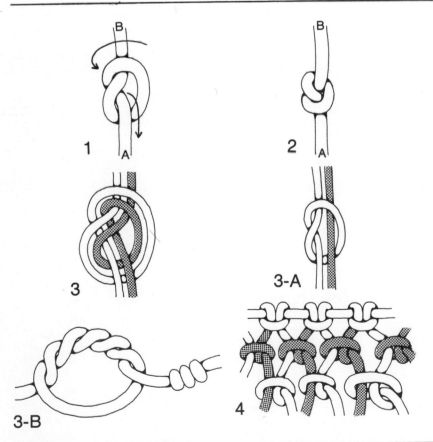

Simplest of all macramé knots, the overhand knot itself requires only one cord yet has several interesting variations. Use it for finishes or filler or in chains.

1. Make a loop with the cord by placing end A over end B; then bring end A from behind B and out through the loop (1).

2. Pull the knot tight (2). Several knots in a row will form a chain.

3. Basic variations of this knot include the use of 2 cords to form a single knot (3); the use of 2 cords, 1 knotted around the other (3-A); and the Monk's Belt knot, in which end A is brought around and through the existing loop several times, then pulled tight to form a barrel-like knot (3-B).

The overhand knot variation shown in figure 4 can be adapted to an overall pattern by tying knots across an entire area, then moving one cord over (to the right or to the left of the knot above) in the next row of knots. Repeat this sequence until the pattern area is complete.

Half Hitch and Double Half Hitch

The half hitch is the first step to forming a double half hitch, one of the two basic macramé knots. A loose, looplike "knot," the half hitch is rarely used by itself; instead, this "knot" can be added to a basic double half hitch to form triple and quadruple half hitches.

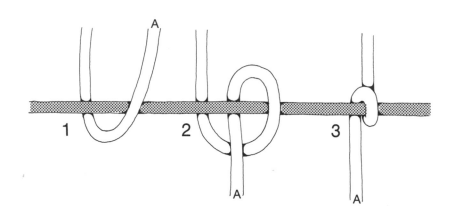

1. Place the midpoint of the working cord behind the holding cord; then bring end A up over the holding cord (1).

2. Pull end A down behind the holding cord and out through the loop that is formed (2); then pull the "knot" tight (3). The half hitch is not secure by itself; it must be repeated to form a snug, somewhat permanent knot.

The double half hitch is just two half hitches knotted in succession, using the same tying cord. Very versatile, this knot can be used to create a variety of special effects.

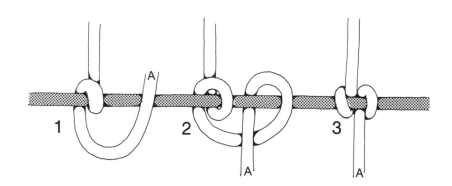

1. To form a double half hitch, follow the steps given for the half hitch; then bring end A back up over the holding cord (1).

2. Pull end A down behind the holding cord and out through the loop formed by the 2 half hitches (2).

3. Pull the end tight to form a completed knot (3).

The placement of the holding cord and the angle at which it is held makes it possible to create many different effects with a succession of double half hitch knots. Horizontal, diagonal, and free-form rows of double half hitches are the basic ingredients for a wide range of macramé patterns.

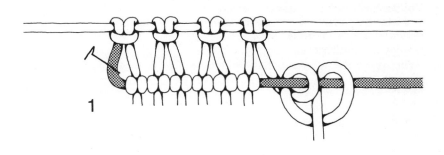

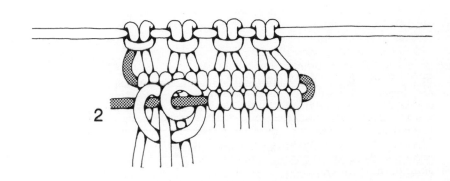

1. Mount the midpoints of 4 cords to form 8 working cords; then, using the far left-hand cord as a holding cord, tie a double half hitch over it with each of the remaining working cords (1).

2. When the last cord has been knotted, turn the holding cord in the opposite direction and knot a row of double half hitches from right to left (2).

3. The first variation possible is the diagonal bar. Either outside working cord may be used as a holding cord if pinned to the working surface just under the mounting knot. When this holding cord is pulled taut at a 45° angle across the other cords and double half hitches are knotted over it, a diagonal row is formed (3).

4. Double half hitch bars are really quite flexible—they'll take on any shape you desire. Just pull the holding cord across the working cords and knot away, varying the direction of the holding cord as you tie (4).

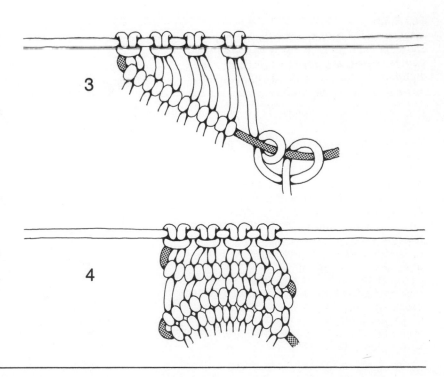

Double Half Hitch Patterns

Double half hitch bars can be combined in a variety of ways to form patterns. The diamond is a basic pattern shape with infinite possibilities.

1. Mount 4 (or more) cords at their midpoints to form 8 working cords. Hold cord E at a 45° angle to the left over cords A, B, C, and D, using them to tie a diagonal row of double half hitches over E (1). Leaving cord E, hold cord D at a 45° angle to the right over cords F, G, and H. Use these cords to tie a diagonal row of double half hitches over D (1-A).

2. At the end of each diagonal row, tie an overhand knot, pinning each securely to the working surface. Hold cord D at a 45° angle to the left over cords F, G, and H; then tie a diagonal row of double half hitches with these cords (2).

Next, hold cord E at a 45° angle to the right over cords A, B, C, and D and tie a diagonal row of double half hitches with these cords to complete the diamond (2-A).

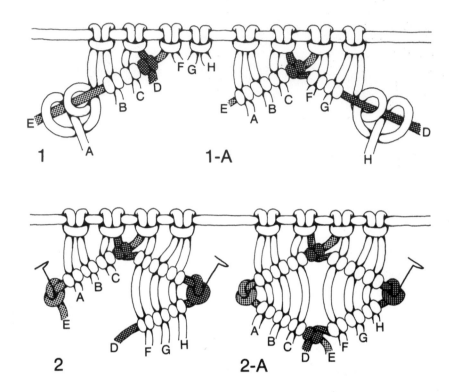

A diagonal cross pattern is formed by using the two outside cords of the pattern unit (comprised of four or more cords) as holding cords for two crossing diagonal rows of double half hitches.

1. Mount 4 cords at their midpoints to make 8 working cords. Tie a row of double half hitches from left to right, using cord A as the holding cord (1); then pin cord B to the working surface and hold it at a 45° angle to the right. With cords C, D, and E, tie a diagonal row of double half hitches (1-A).

2. Pin cord A to the working surface and hold it at a 45° angle to the left; with cords H through C, tie a diagonal row of double half hitches, using cord B at the crossing point (2).

3. Complete the cross by tying the remainder of the diagonal row to the right with cords F, G, and H (2-A).

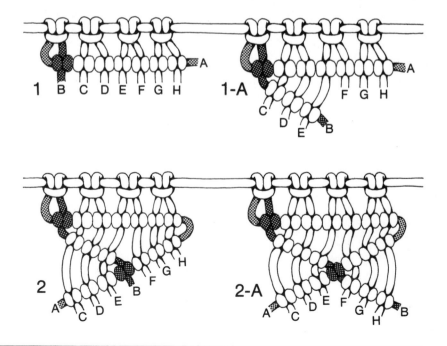

Half Hitch and Double Half Hitch Chains

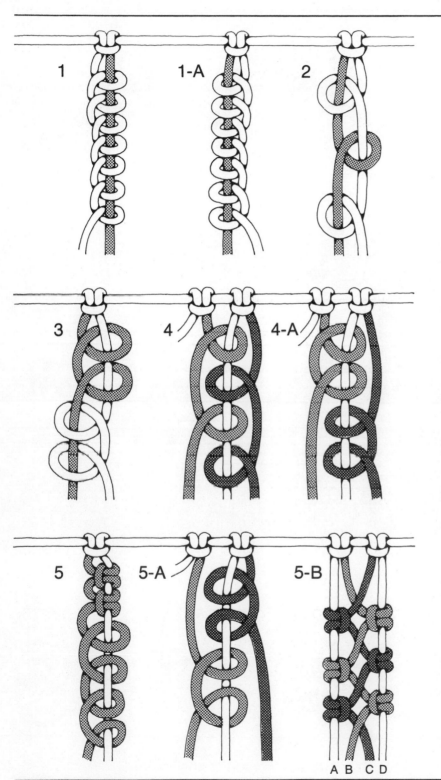

1   1-A   2

3   4   4-A

5   5-A   5-B

A B C D

Chains are decorative fillers made by tying variations of the same knot down two or more working cords. The basic half hitch chain and a number of variations appear at left.

1. Mount 2 cords at their midpoints to form 4 working cords to be used as needed. Put the left cord over and around the right cord and out through the loop that is formed. Repeat several times to form a chain that twists to the right (1). For a twist to the left, loop the right cord around the left (1-A).

2. This variation uses 2 cords alternately looping around each other in half hitch knots (2).

3. Based on variation 2, this 2-cord chain is formed by looping the left cord around the right cord in 2 half hitch knots and then using the right cord to loop 2 half hitch knots around the left cord (3).

4. Three working cords are needed for this pair of half hitch chains. The 1st chain is formed when the left cord is looped around a center cord alternately with the right cord (4). For the 2nd chain (4-A), the left cord is looped twice around the center cord, followed by the right cord looped twice around the center cord.

5. Similar to the mounting knot, the Lark's Head chain can use from 2 to 8 working cords. The basic chain is formed when 1 cord is tied in a series of Lark's Head knots over a 2nd cord (5). The 3-cord version of this knot utilizes a center cord over which Lark's Head knots are tied alternately by the left and by the right cords (5-A).

Four cords are used for a latticework effect, the 2 outside cords (A and D) acting as anchors or holding cords for Lark's Head knots tied first with cord C over cord A, then with cord B over cord D (5-B). Chains with more cords than this are variations on these 3 basic chains.

Shaping with Double Half Hitches

You can go beyond the limitations of parallel borders in macramé by using these methods for making color changes, sharp angles, or three-dimensional shapes.

These instructions can be reversed and the number of cords changed to alter shapes, spirals, angles, and color changes.

1. For an example of how color changes can be made, at their midpoints mount 2 cords of 1 color and 2 cords of a contrasting color to make 8 working cords. Make 7 horizontal rows of double half hitches, working from left to right and moving over 1 holding cord at a time, to form a triangular shape (1).

At that point begin working double half hitches downward along the right edge, starting with cord A as a vertical holding cord; also use cords B through F as holding cords to form a shape as in 1-A. To continue the angle of the pattern, begin to use the bottom cords as holding cords (1-B). To reverse the angle, work back in the opposite direction (1-C).

2. Other color changes are possible when the vertical double half hitch is introduced (2).

3. To form a sharp-angled zigzag shape (multiples of which can be interlocked), start with 4 working cords and knot them as in 1 and 1-A; but continue to use this method until all 4 working cords have been used as tying cords to form a shape as in 3. Then change directions and angle back as in 1-C until all 4 cords have been returned to their original locations (3-A). Repeat for zigzag.

4. Three-dimensional shapes, such as the pagoda bell pull project shown on page 47, are made possible by starting with working cords knotted to the point shown in illustration 1. Then the entire shape is turned on its side (4) and again knotted from left to right until a 2nd triangular shape, or side, is formed (4-A). Continue to turn the piece and knot triangles to form a spiral.

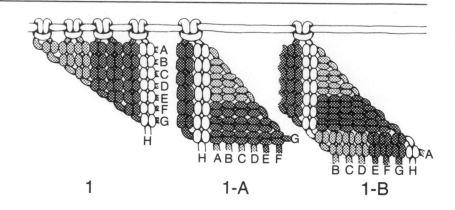

1   1-A   1-B

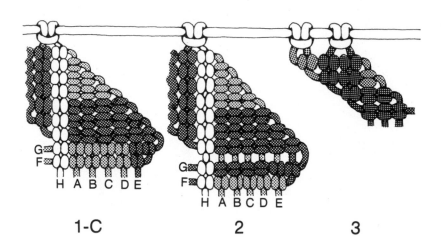

1-C   2   3

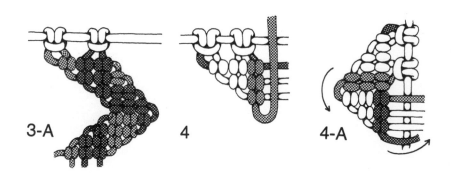

3-A   4   4-A

Vertical Double Half Hitch and Alternate Diagonal Double Half Hitch

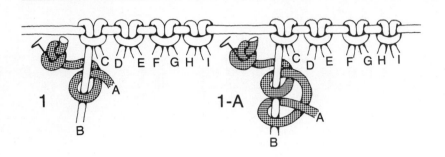

1   1-A

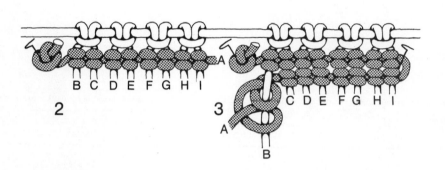

2   3

For textural variation, shaping, and color changes, the vertical double half hitch is an important knotting variation. The holding cord becomes the tying cord, and all working cords become holding cords.

1. Mount 4 cords at their midpoints and pin cord A to the working surface. Bring cord B over cord A and knot a double half hitch over B with cord A (1 and 1-A).

2. Pull the knot tight; then complete a row of vertical double half hitches, beginning each knot with the horizontal tying cord A under each vertical holding cord (2).

3. For a 2nd row of knots, pin cord A to the working surface and place it behind cord I. Pull cord A around behind cord I and through the loop formed. Bring end A down, around, and behind I again; then pull A out through the loop formed. Repeat this procedure until all knots in the 2nd row are formed (3).

A seemingly random, nubby pattern emerges when the directions of rows of diagonally tied double half hitches alternate from left to right.

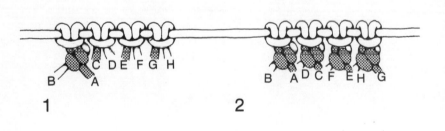

1   2

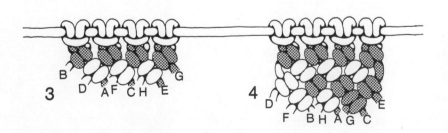
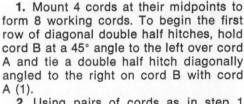

3   4

1. Mount 4 cords at their midpoints to form 8 working cords. To begin the first row of diagonal double half hitches, hold cord B at a 45° angle to the left over cord A and tie a double half hitch diagonally angled to the right on cord B with cord A (1).

2. Using pairs of cords as in step 1 work from left to right, tying 4 diagonal double half hitch knots in all (2).

3. For the 2nd row, work from left to right again, but this time leave the far left cord (B) free. With cord D, tie a double half hitch diagonally angled to the left over cord A. Complete the row by tying 2 more knots in the same manner (3).

4. For an overall pattern, continue to alternate rows in this way. Eventually a nubby, random appearance will become visible throughout the area (4).

Square Knot and Alternate Square Knot

The square knot is one of the two basic macramé knots (the double half hitch is the other). Variations and patterns occur when you add tying and holding cords and combine this knot with other knots.

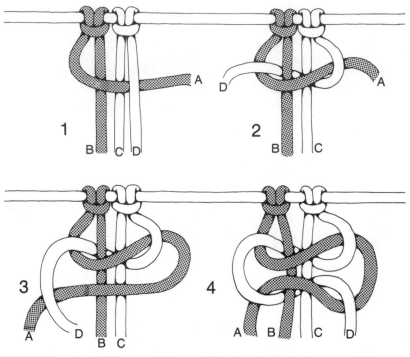

1. Mount 2 cords at their midpoints to make 4 working cords. Keep the 2 middle cords stationary and work with cords A and D. Pull cord A across cords B and C and under cord D (1).

2. Then bring cord D under cords C and B and over cord A, coming up through the loop formed between cord B and cord A (2).

3. Next, bring cord A over cords C and B and under cord D (3). To complete the knot, pull cord D under cords B and C, then up behind cord A and out through the loop formed by A (4).

4. Pull the knot tight. If you want to reverse the direction of the knot, start with cord D.

The alternate square knot pattern is formed when holding cords and tying cords are exchanged in succeeding rows of knots. This knot can have a lacy appearance or a weavelike texture, depending on how tightly it is knotted.

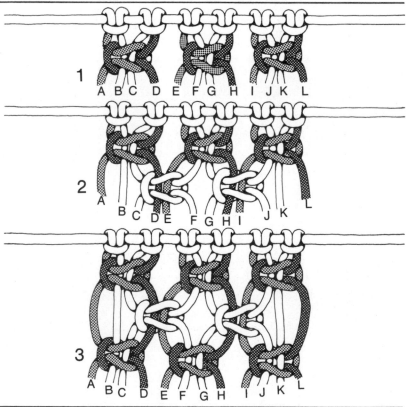

1. Mount 6 cords at their midpoints to make 12 working cords; then tie 3 square knots, using 4 cords for each knot (1).

2. Pull aside cords A and B, as well as cords K and L; then divide the remaining 8 cords into 2 groups of 4 cords each. Tie a square knot with each group of 4 cords (2). In this row, working cords from row 1 become holding cords and holding cords from row 1 become working cords.

3. Bring down cords A, B, K, and L, incorporating them again into the knotting. As in row 1, knot 3 square knots, using 4 cords for each knot (3) to create an overall pattern.

Half Knot and Square Knot Chains

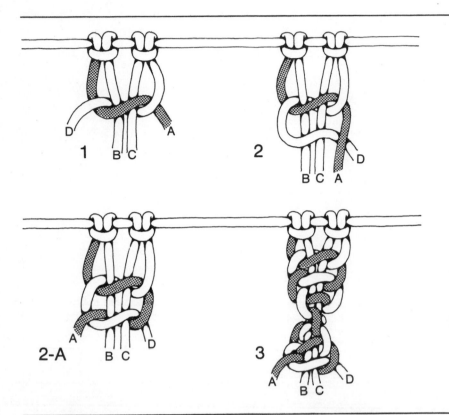

A basic variation on the square knot chain, the half knot chain has a natural twist to the right or to the left, depending on which working cord is used first.

1. Mount 2 cords at their midpoints to form 4 working cords. Tie a half knot as in figure 1, starting with cord A going over cords B and C and under D. Cord D goes under cords C and B and over A.

2. To continue, again start from the left, which is now cord D, and place D *over* cords B and C, then under A (2). Bring cord A under D, behind C and B and out between B and D (2-A).

3. Repeat steps 1 and 2 in order several times, and you will notice a definite twist to the right in the chain (3). Don't let the twisting chain confuse you about which cord to start with; always use the cord closest to the side from which you originally began the chain.

4. For a twist to the left, start with the right-hand cord.

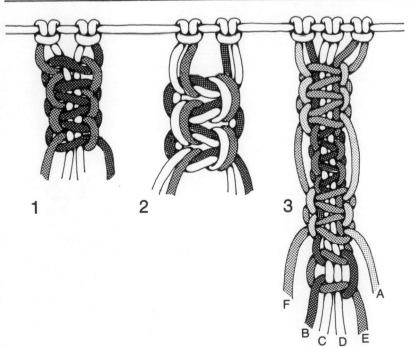

The square knot can be used for chains, as well as for an overall pattern. You can vary this basic chain design by adding or subtracting holding cords or tying cords from original chain design.

1. Create the basic square knot chain by tying a series of square knots with the same 4 cords (as in figure 1).

2. A basic variation of this chain is the use of 4 working cords and no holding cords (2).

3. Another variation uses 6 cords; the 2 outside cords (A and F) are used to tie a series of square knots over the 4 center cords. Then cords A and F are pinned to the side while cords B and E are used as working cords to tie a series of square knots over cords C and D. These knots are followed by a repeat of the 1st element, cords A and F tying square knots over cords B, C, D, and E (3).

Bobble Knot and Berry Pattern

Three-dimensional sculptural forms add textural interest to macraméd surfaces. The bobble (or popcorn) knot is a simple means of forming a knobby surface. It's comprised of a square knot chain pulled up and back into itself to form a ball (or bobble) shape.

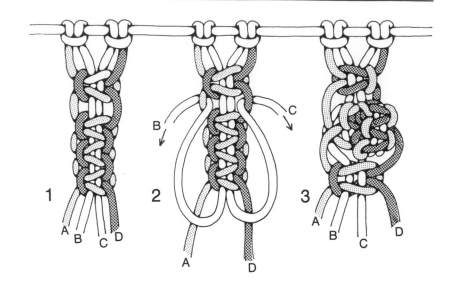

1. Mount 2 cords at their midpoints to form 4 working cords. Tie 1 square knot, leave a small space; then tie a series of 3 (or more if the bobble is to be large) closely spaced square knots (1).

2. Pass cords B and C up and back through the space made by separating the 1st square knot from those that follow (2).

3. To form a tight ball, pull down on cords B and C until the square knot chain doubles back on itself and forms a loop-like bobble. With A and D, tie a firm square knot directly under the bobble (3).

Another knoblike pattern used for surface detail work, the berry pattern (also called "hobnail") is slightly more complicated than the bobble but has a more definitively shaped appearance.

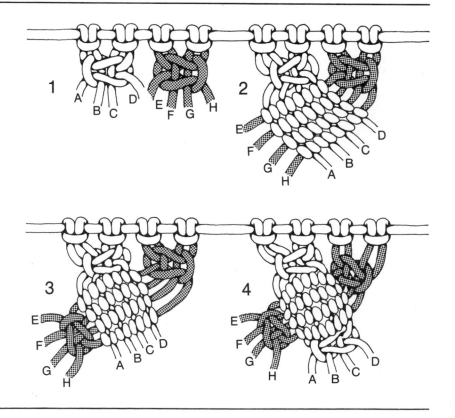

1. Mount 4 cords at their midpoints to form 8 working cords. Divide them into 2 sets of 4 cords each and tie 2 square knots (1).

2. Use cords E, F, G, and H as holding cords to tie 4 diagonal rows of double half hitches from upper right to lower left (2) with cords A, B, C, and D.

3. Using cords E, F, G, and H, tie a square knot at the left side of the berry, using cords F and G as holding cords and cords E and H as working cords. Push up against the square knot and tie it firmly to round out the berry shape (3).

4. To complete the pattern, tie a 2nd square knot at the right side of the berry with cords B and C as holding cords and cords A and D as working cords (4). Firm up the shape as in step 3 to complete.

Josephine Knot and Turk's-head Knot

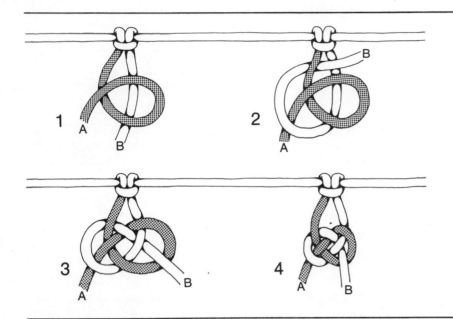

A decorative knot used quite often in belts and jewelry, the Josephine knot can be a small, delicate filler or a bold, almost graphic statement, depending upon the number of cords used to tie the knot.

1. Mount 1 cord at its midpoint to form 2 working cords. Loop cord A and place this loop over cord B (1).

2. Pull the end of cord B over, then under, cord A (2).

3. Bring cord end B down over the top of the looped portion of cord A, under cord B itself, and out over the outside of the looped portion of cord A (3).

4. Pull both cord ends to tighten the knot (4). To make a larger, more dramatic knot, use groups of 2 or more cords for A and for B.

Use the Turk's-head knot to make buttons, closures, or rings. Or use it as a decorative ending for hanging cords.

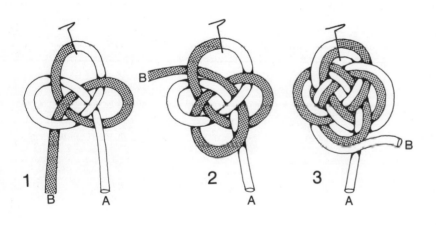

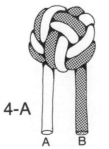

1. Cut one 30-inch-long cord and pin it to the working surface 10 inches from end A and 20 inches from end B, allowing both cord ends to hang free. (If cord end A is attached to your macramé piece, work with this page turned upside down and pin down the cord 10 inches below the point of attachment.) Tie a Josephine knot (see above) near the pinned fold of the cord so that the fold forms a 3rd loop (1).

2. Bring end B over end A and up parallel to cord A; then begin to follow A with end B around the flat Josephine knot (2).

3. Continue to follow along the original loops in the knot until every part of the knot has 2 cords and end B is again over end A (3). Repeat this process as many times as you wish; each repeat will enlarge the knot.

4. To form a ring, place your index fingers through the center opening of the flat knot and pull outward (4). For a tight ball, place a small marble or bead in the center of the ring and pull on all cords in the ring until they close snugly around the bead core (4-A).

Picots

Picots—lacelike decorative elements added to the starting point of a macramé piece—are formed before or during the mounting of working cords. Directions for several styles are given at right.

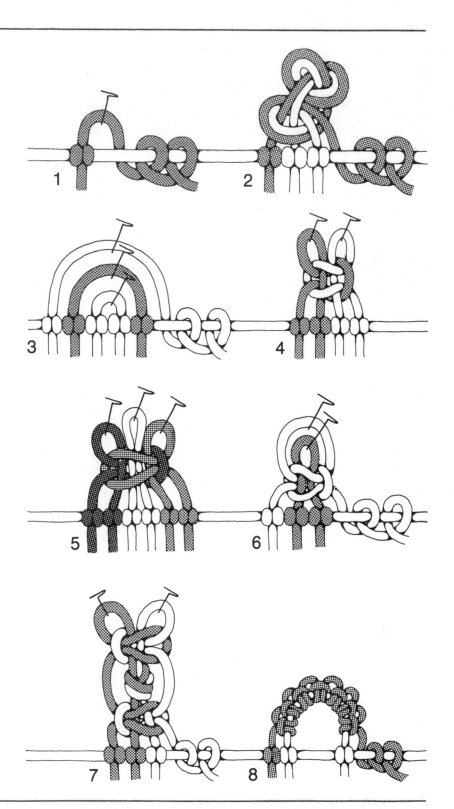

1. Form this picot by double half hitching both ends of a working cord slightly below its midpoint to the mounting cord (1).

2. Make this picot by mounting 2 cords, then looping them as 1 and remounting them as shown in figure 2.

3. The midpoints of 3 successive cords are pinned just above the mounting cord, then mounted from the center out to form this rainbow-shaped picot (3).

4. Begin this picot by pinning the midpoints of 2 cords next to each other above the mounting cord. Using the two central ends as an anchor, tie a square knot with the outer ends; then pull the knot tight and mount all 4 cords (4).

5. Arrange the midpoints of 3 separate cords in a pyramid, the center midpoint pinned above the outer midpoints. Tie a square knot over the central cords with the 2 outer cords; then mount all 6 ends (5).

6. Pin the midpoints of 2 cords, 1 above the other, to the working surface. Use the lower cord as an anchor for a square knot tied with the ends of the upper cord; then mount all 4 cords (6).

7. Make picot 4 but, before mounting it, tie an overhand knot with the 2 central cords; then tie a 2nd square knot below the overhand knot (7). Mount ends.

8. Mount the midpoints of 2 cords; then use the left-hand cord to tie a series of 6 or more Lark's Head knots over the right-hand cord (8). Mount the 2 remaining ends.

Wrapping and Plaiting

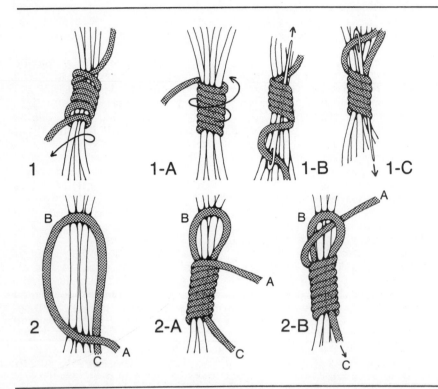

1   1-A   1-B   1-C

2   2-A   2-B

Wrapping can be used to join cords, finish ends off, or add color or unusual textural areas to your macramé work.

1. For soft, pliant cords, this method works best: group 2 or more cords into a bundle; then use one of the cords to wrap or cover this bundle, starting from the top or the bottom and working down (1) or up (1-A). When the wrapping is long enough, thread the cord end through the eye of a blunt tapestry needle and use it to pull the cord end through the wrapped coil (1-B and 1-C). Cut off cord end.

2. When heavy or slippery cords are being used, group them into a bundle; then cut a separate cord about 36 inches long. Loop the cord next to the bundle and bring end A across the bundle and end C (2). Begin wrapping with A, covering the bundle *and* loop B, working upward until only about an inch of loop B is left free (2-A). Thread end A through loop B and pull down on end C until A and B are pulled inside (2-B). Cut off cord end.

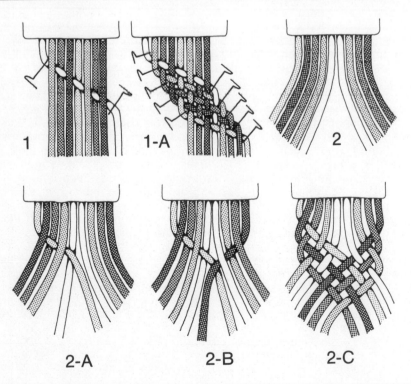

1   1-A   2

2-A   2-B   2-C

Though employed with macramé in the form of belts, straps, handles, or pattern filler, plaiting is actually a fancy form of braiding. Two versions of this method, flat and French, are shown at left.

1. For flat plaiting, cut an even number of cords, each 1½ times longer than the desired finished length. Line them up along one edge of your working surface and secure them with a clamp.

Weave the far left cord through the remaining cords (1), using T-pins as shown.

Working from left to right, continue to weave each far left cord through the remaining cords, incorporating at the right edge all previously woven cords (1-A).

2. For French plaiting, repeat step 1 but use an odd number of cords divided into 2 groups, the left-hand group having the extra cord (2).

Follow figures 2-A, 2-B, and 2-C, working individual cords alternately left to right, right to left. Continue in this manner, incorporating all previously woven cords into the design at the center (2-C).

Working Techniques

When you're "building" a project, you need more than just the basic know-how of tying macramé knots and patterns—these are only the raw materials. To join them into a working unit, you must also apply special techniques. This chapter offers you a selection of methods for starting, finishing, enlarging, diminishing, shaping, and fastening your macramé projects. Some of the methods are particularly suited to specific types of macramé; others can be employed in almost any project.

Starting from a point

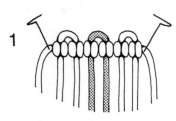

1

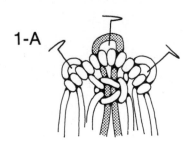

1-A

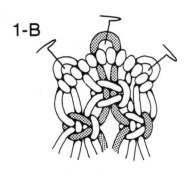

1-B

Choosing Working Surfaces

Is your macramé project long or short? Is it wide or narrow, flat or three-dimensional? Will you carry it with you or work on it exclusively at home? Consider all of these factors when you're choosing a working surface.

Small projects (jewelry and belts, for example) are most easily constructed on clipboards or on small pieces of fiberboard or foam. A lap board is a good choice for bracelets, chokers, and narrow belts.

Larger projects, such as purses, pillow covers, or small hangings, require a larger working area. Since fiberboard is available in any number of sizes, it ranks high as a larger working surface. Stretcher bar frames in various sizes can also be used, though they don't give the support of fiberboard.

Three-dimensional pieces require individual solutions. Hats are most successfully constructed on a wig or hat stand. Clothing, though, can be approached in two ways: one-piece construction (using a dressmaker's form for support) or pattern-piece construction. The latter breaks a design down into individual patterns, such as sleeve or bodice pieces; these are pinned or drawn onto the working surface, and the knotting is worked to fit the shape of the pattern.

Plant hangers and three-dimensional sculptures can be suspended from hooks or bars attached to a ceiling beam or to the overhead portion of a door jamb. Or they can be worked in stages on a large, flat piece of fiberboard or foam. If the project is a specific shape, it can be worked over a jig, or form. Jigs can be adapted from existing jars, boxes, or pillows; special jigs can be cut from plywood or fiberboard.

If you plan to make a valance, window covering, or doorway curtain, it's best to knot the project "on location" to assure proper fit and design suitability. If you can't attach your work directly to the window or door frame, devise a method for mounting your cords on a removable support that can be hung or set into the existing door or window frame.

Beginning a Project

Once you've decided to knot a specific item, the next decision you'll face will be choosing a suitable way to begin. Will you attach your cords to something or will they be self-supporting? If you decide to use a support, what will it be, and how will the cords be attached?

Macramé mounts vary with the type of project. Metal or wooden rings and hoops, bars and dowels, driftwood and tree branches, wire armatures and wooden frames, even hole-punched leather (note the cape on the facing page) or fabric can be used as starting points.

Cords can easily be mounted in the conventional way (see page 11) or attached with double half hitches at any point on the mount. Some mounts, such as driftwood and purse handles, will require drilling or punching in order to hold cords. Other mounts can take the form of purchased belt buckles, beads, or jump-ring closures. These are frequently used in the construction of jewelry and belts.

Some projects won't require a separate mount; rather, they will transform the mounting cord into a working cord, eventually incorporating it into the body of the piece. Since no discernible starting point will exist if this method is used, a piece may be started either at the middle or at one end. Belts, jewelry, purses, some garments, and some decorative macramé can be worked in this manner, as can a number of three-dimensional constructions.

Purses, belts, and watch straps will often begin at a point which later forms an end or a flap. One method for starting from a point is shown in figure 1 at left; the following starting methods are illustrated on the facing page: self-mounting cord (fig. 1), self-loop cord (fig. 2), continuous neck cord (fig. 3), loop-and-bead mount (fig. 4), and the jump-ring mount (fig. 5). Self-mounting cords and self-loop cord mounts can be used for almost any type of macramé; the three latter methods are used almost exclusively for jewelry making.

Starting from the center is a technique employed most frequently for knotting

Leather cape *with punch-mounted macramé fringe. Design: Lois Ericson.*

Purse started *from a pointed flap. Design: Gerta Wingerd.* **Close-up** *of belt point.*

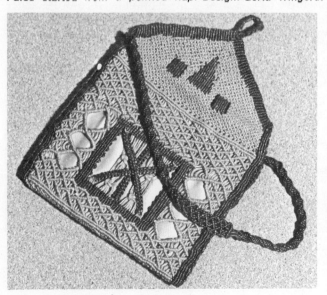

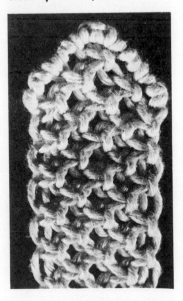

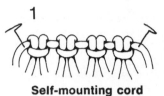

Self-mounting cord

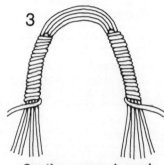

Self-loop cord

Continuous neck cord

Rope Core

Loop-and-bead mount

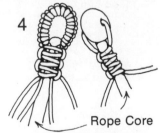

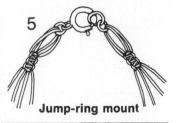

Jump-ring mount

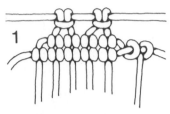

Adding new holding cords

**Adding new cord
to a square knot chain**

**Adding new cords
between square knots**

Adding new working cord

belts or jewelry. The unused portions of the cords can be draped over the top of the working surface or held in a paper bag, as shown below, right, on this page. Starting from the midpoint of a piece of jewelry often means beginning at the point where the pendant and the neck strands meet. A good example of this approach is shown at lower left on this page.

Adding or Subtracting Cords

Changing the size of a project, filling in or removing an open area, introducing or eliminating color, adding extra cord where the original working cord has run short, or deleting cords where they are no longer needed—these are situations that require specific solutions. Following—and illustrated at left—are several possibilities.

To enlarge the dimensions of a project, you can mount new cord lengths in available spaces, increase width by adding in new working cords in the form of holding cords (fig. 1), add new cord to the core of a square knot chain (fig. 2) or between 2 alternating square knots (fig. 3), or add new working cord by knotting the short end of the cord into the holding cord (fig. 4).

Extra space can be made for new cords in a double half hitch pattern area row by knotting triple or quadruple half hitches in the preceding row. In a square knot pattern area, cords can be added between individual alternating square knots.

When working or holding cords run short, new cords can be discreetly introduced in several ways; all are shown on the facing page. In a row of double half hitches, you can lengthen the holding cord by adding in new cord as shown in figure 1. Use this method also when a double half hitch working cord is running short (see fig. 4, this page). If the holding cord of any square knot runs short, add a new length of cord as in figure 2, this page. If a square knot working cord is short, exchange it for one of its longer holding cords (fig. 2, page 27) and then add a new holding cord.

Vertical double half hitches tend to use up cord very quickly. To lengthen a rapidly diminishing working cord, cut the existing cord to 3 inches after a completed row; then add in a new working cord to begin the next row, leaving a 3-inch end free at the start. These two ends can be glued to the back of the work when it is completed.

If a too-short cord is made of firm material, it can be spliced to a new cord with glue or thread. To splice with glue, cut both cords at an angle with a sharp knife, dip each end into glue, and bind the ends together with thread until dry.

To sew cords together, cut the ends at an angle and hold them together; then, with matching thread, stitch through one end at a point directly below the splice and wrap the thread up over both cord ends, keeping it in the spaces between the plies of the coil. Stitch through the

Graceful oriental necklace of waxed nylon and jade was begun where the pendant meets the neck strands. Design: Grace Chinn.

Loose cord ends can be held in a plastic or paper bag to keep them from tangling while you knot a piece begun from the center.

end above the splice and knot off the thread.

Cords will sometimes need to be eliminated, either gradually or suddenly. Here's how. The simplest way to drop a cord is to knot over it, leaving it hanging unused at the back of the piece where it can later be cut off. Knotting off is a means of gradually dropping cords by overhand knotting each unwanted cord and clipping off the excess end (fig. 3).

Another method for gradual elimination is the use of two or more cords as one working or holding cord until the extra cord(s) can be safely clipped off.

To abruptly eliminate a group of cords, try the cumulative edge method: group the excess cords into a bundle and use them all as one holding cord for a row of double half hitches, clipping off one excess end every three or four knots (fig. 4) until all cords but one are eliminated.

Three-dimensional Shaping

Working in more than two dimensions requires planning and some experience.

Unless plans are made to gradually introduce new cords, either your project will become very open and structurally weak or its size will be limited to the general dimensions of the mount you use.

To provide extra support and more cord-mounting surface as the piece grows, you can add new mountings, such as the hoops in the tiered hanging shown at the lower left on this page. Covering existing three-dimensional objects—such as bottles, flowerpots, and lamp shades—is easier than creating a sculpture from scratch.

Basketry techniques will produce any number of three-dimensional shapes, such as the hanging shown in the photograph at lower right on this page; refer to the basket project on page 54 for more detailed information on this subject.

Overknotting is a method of forcing holding cords into a tight, random pattern by experimenting with the tension, placement, and number of double and vertical half hitches knotted within a given area. This is a freeform approach, and the best way to understand it is to experiment with it; an example is shown on page 28.

Plant hangers are probably the most

1

Lengthening the holding cord

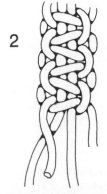

2

Exchanging a working cord for a holding cord

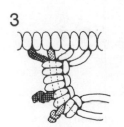

3

Knotting off unwanted cord ends

Three-dimensional macramé sculpture *in tiers grows with the addition of wooden hoops in graduated sizes. Design: Jacee Johnson.*

Coil work *incorporates double half hitches, wrapping, beads, and fringe to produce this natural basket form. Design: Susan Lehman.*

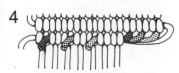

4

Cumulative edge method for eliminating cords

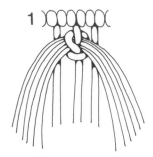

Thickening fringe

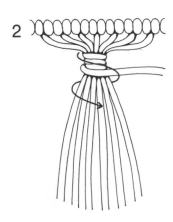

Wrapping fringe

familiar form of three-dimensional macramé. They can be started in two dimensions, then expanded to a third dimension. The addition of hoops or bars will accomplish this; so will division of the working cords into chains that are later regrouped into one bundle to form a loose "cradle" for the flowerpot. Both solutions are shown on the facing page. Other approaches are covered in the projects given on pages 43 and 59.

One of the most popular macramé projects is the covered bottle, an easy accomplishment if you keep the following points in mind: 1) Start at the neck of the bottle with a circular self-mount; 2) Keep knotting tight, evenly spaced, and consistent; 3) Add cords as needed to conform to the swell of the lower bottle; 4) Finish off the bottom in a diminishing concentric spiral of double half hitch rows, clipping off and tucking under cord ends as the spiral decreases (see facing page).

Purses can be considered three-dimensional. There are basically three ways to shape a purse: 1) Two separate pieces are knotted, then later sewn together or attached at the sides to a continuous side/shoulder strap (see facing page); 2) One long piece is knotted, then folded in half and joined at the sides; 3) The bag is worked over a jig for an initial three-dimensional shape (see below).

Finishing Techniques

The natural finish for a macramé piece is fringe, but if this doesn't suit your design, consider these alternate treatments.

Existing fringe can be altered in several ways: 1) Thicken the fringe by adding extra lengths of cord as in figure 1, at left; 2) Divide fringe into bunches and wrap them into bundles (see fig. 2); 3) Divide fringe into tassels either by wrapping slightly below the point at which a bundle of cords has been attached (fig. 2, at left) or by using a gathering knot to bind each bundle (fig. 1, page 29).

Where you don't want fringe, cut cord ends to not less than 1 inch, depending on the size and pliability of the cord, and either glue all ends to the wrong side of the project with white glue or weave the fringe ends back into the body of the piece, keeping them to the wrong side (fig. 2, page 29).

To join edges where there is fringe, simply knot together the fringe from both sides. Where there is no fringe (the sides

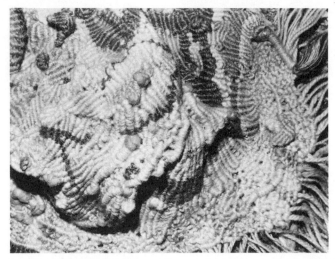

Sculptural quality of "Meteora," *a small hanging, is emphasized by overknotting (see page 27). Colors are added, worked through the piece, and gradually removed; the technique is similar to that used in the basket project on page 54. Design: Marion Ferri.*

A purse jig *is made from an empty oatmeal box that has been filled with dry sand and taped shut with masking tape. The bag will have no side seams when worked with this method since knotting continues uninterrupted around the jig.*

of a piece or edges that are glued or woven), edges can be either knotted together with an extra cord (fig. 3, this page) or interlaced with an extra cord (fig. 4, this page).

Some cords—especially nylon, rayon, and cotton cable—will need to have their ends sealed in some manner to prevent them from unraveling. Tie an overhand knot at the end of each cord or (for cotton or rayon) dip cord ends into white glue.

Nylon cord ends can be melted into a ball over a match flame, but be very careful—they can burn your fingers.

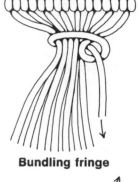

1

Bundling fringe

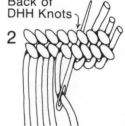

Back of DHH Knots

2

Woven edge finish

Bottle bottom *is tightly covered with a decreasing spiral of double half hitches from which cords are gradually eliminated.*

Knotted shoulder strap band *can be attached along both sides of a knotted handbag to add width and support. Design: Gerta Wingerd.*

3

Joining edges of square knotted projects

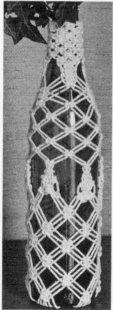

Covered bottles *can be started at the neck for complete coverage* **(left),** *or at the shoulder to avoid adding extra cords* **(right).** *Designs: left, Alison Jones; right, E. R. Vorenkamp.*

Plant hangers *are sculptural macramé. Support pots by joined cords* **(left)** *or by hoops knotted into the hanging* **(right).** *Designs: left, Winkie Fordney; right, Esther Parada.*

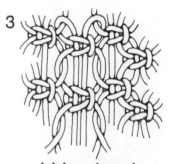
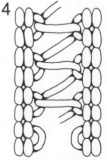

4

Joining edges of double half hitch knotted projects

Design and Color for Macramé

If you yearn to design a truly unique macramé project of your own or to alter one of the projects included in this book, the following information on design and color will help guide you through the decision-making process.

Planning Your Project

Asking yourself a few questions is a logical prelude to actually beginning a project. What shall I make? What size will it be? What color or colors would be suitable? What materials will give it the correct texture and body?

Try to keep the size of the project and the complexity of the design and the knotting pattern in balance with your abilities and the amount of time you'll want to spend working on the piece.

Because of its flexible nature, macramé can use color in very simple or very complex ways, depending on the manner in which a knotting progression is developed. Unless you have a great deal of experience with color, the best rule to follow is this: keep it simple.

If the knotting pattern of the piece is its most important element, then limit the number of colors. If color movement and blending are paramount to the success of the project, choose shades that either complement each other or blend for a harmonious overall effect.

The type of project you want to make, its size, the colors you'll use, and the knotting progression you'll follow—all of these decisions will influence your choice of materials. If, for example, you decide to make a macramé drapery for a window, choose materials that are thick enough to prevent the knotting process from taking months on end. The materials should also be colorfast so they won't fade in sunlight (primary or strong colors have a greater tendency to fade than do natural shades).

When selecting materials for use in articles that will either receive a great deal of wear or require occasional cleaning, check for shrinkage, colorfastness, shedding properties, and (in the case of apparel) comfort. A jute vest may be bright and bouncy in appearance but impossible to wear because of the roughness of the fiber.

To prevent bagging or a droopy look, avoid soft, stretchy cord or yarn in a garment unless it is closely knotted or has some extra support.

Planning may seem less important to you than the actual knotting process. But, as you will see, many mistakes and problems can be prevented if all factors are thought through ahead of time.

The Concept of Design in Macramé

Though any number of interesting knots can be used to construct a macramé piece, the manner in which these knots are combined can make a startling difference. For satisfactory results in macramé a simple appreciation of design basics is necessary. A well-planned piece will combine all elements of design into a harmonious whole that could become unbalanced if anything were added or taken away (the purse at right is a good example).

Design can be reduced to three basic elements: line, shape, and space. Though design is consciously used in handcrafted or machinecrafted articles, its pure form exists in nature.

Take time to really observe the things around you that go unnoticed in day-to-day life: the linear qualities of tree trunks and limbs, shape in the form of a squirrel or bird, space in the delicate web of a spider (note the bottom photographs on page 31). Size, density, texture, and color add dimension to these basic factors.

Size, of course, should be appropriate to the function and placement of the article; density will determine its weight, drape, and flow. Texture and color are used to guide the hand and the eye.

A smooth texture and monochromatic color scheme enhance the knots used in a project (see the lower left photograph on page 32 for an example of this approach); a rough, ropy, or nubby surface, though, will have the effect of emphasizing the overall form of the piece (as in the upper right photograph on page 31). Color can be used sparingly (to highlight only certain pattern areas) or boldly (to set a mood or to create a visual theme).

To learn more about such qualities as texture, density, and color, select several macramé works that appeal to you from the gallery on page 74. Break them down into their basic elements. Start with the knotting patterns used and figure out how they have been combined. Then go on to isolate and explore the uses to which line, space, and shape are put.

Note the natural divisions characteristic to macramé; horizontal, vertical, and diagonal lines or pattern areas are the most common. Curves, circles, and undulating lines require a sure hand and some previous knotting experience (see the lower right photograph on page 32).

When you sit down to think out a project, keep in mind the knowledge you've gained from these explorations. There are two ways to work: from a plan or cartoon or in a freeform manner. A cartoon can be as sketchy or as detailed as you wish. Usually it's executed on graph paper ruled with a certain number of squares to the inch and includes a sketch marked with information on size, colors to be used, and any knotting or shaping details pertinent to the construction of the project.

A freeform approach, on the other hand, requires greater versatility and foresight on the part of the artist. Greater spontaneity in the finished work is your reward for taking chances with your design idea and the materials you plan to use (note the example at lower center on page 33).

Freeform macramé is a medium demanding discipline and patience; if something doesn't work, be prepared to reknot the offending area until it satisfies you. This discipline also calls for shunning the stock solutions to standard problems. Being creative in your approach to problem solving will elevate your work to the plane of individuality (see the center photograph on page 32).

Using Color in Macramé

Color is a very personal aspect of design. Often people will have a natural sense of color without knowing any of the so-called color "rules." Though it's not necessary to memorize rules, it *is* important to have

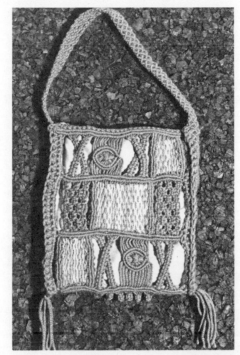

Shoulder bag *displays basic design elements in proper balance* **(left).** *Overall form of amber bead necklace* **(right)** *is emphasized by a nubby surface texture. Designs: left, Gerta Wingerd; right, Paul Johnson.*

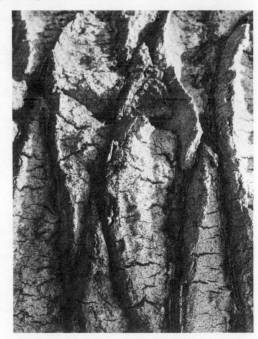

Rough ridges *of an aged palm tree* **(right)** *could have inspired the tightly knotted rows present in the hanging at left. Design: Marion Ferri.*

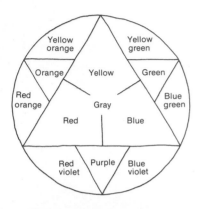

a basic knowledge of what color is, what it can do, and how you can apply it to the craft of macramé.

Understanding the composition of colors gives you confidence in your medium; it allows you to employ colors so that they work well in your macramé projects.

Color is best understood in terms of a color wheel (shown at left). The wheel positions colors in an order that shows how each color relates to its adjacent and its complementary colors. The primary colors of red, blue, and yellow (shown at the center of the wheel) can be combined to make the secondary colors of orange, green, and purple. These colors, in turn, can be mixed with their adjacent hues to make tertiary colors, such as red violet, yellow green, or blue violet.

This principle of mixing certain hues to achieve new colors can be applied directly to macramé. Experiment by twisting several lengths of red and yellow cord together; you'll find that the resulting cord appears to be orange.

The color wheel has what is termed "warm" and "cool" sides. Oranges and reds are considered warm colors; blues and greens fall into the category designated as cool colors. Because warm colors are associated with sunlight and brightness, they appear to be closer and larger than they actually are. Cool colors, on the other hand, tend to recede. These are hues associated with water and shadows.

The texture of the knotting cords will also play a part in altering the appearance of colors. Different surface qualities and diameters of cord will create different high

Simplicity in design and color *can be very effective, as displayed in this double half hitched cascade necklace. Brightly colored wool trimmed with fringe adds drama. Design: Lois Ericson.*

Beaded chains of knots *are gathered into a necklace so natural it might have grown rather than having been constructed. Design: Joyce Barnes.*

Doorway drapery *presents the complex problem of working cords into the center of a circle and out again. Design: Virginia Summit.*

and low areas on the face of the piece, adding subtle shadings to an area that would otherwise appear as solid color.

Effectively using color in your macramé can be handled in three ways. The first is to add in new colors at any point along the way by some of the techniques explained on page 26. Other colors can be removed or simply held back in a certain area—just leave them hanging at the back of the piece until they are again needed.

A second method is to manipulate existing color (the color that was originally knotted into the piece) across the face of the project in a number of ways. Sinnets and chains can move colors; each cord in a two or a four-cord unit can be a different color and can be interchanged as a working or a holding cord to either display or conceal its hue (see below, left).

The Cavandoli knot is a classic approach to using more than one color in a specifically knotted pattern area. The color of the holding cord can be varied to introduce color variety (see below, right).

A third way of using color is to move it out of its original alignment by using chains, sinnets, or diagonal rows of double half hitches. Keep color groups together but work them across or through one another for visual interest.

Think about the colors that will surround the finished project when it is displayed. For contrast, choose colors opposite on the color wheel from those appearing in the setting. For a blended effect, use related colors instead.

Remember—colors are never just ugly or beautiful; it's how you use them that counts.

  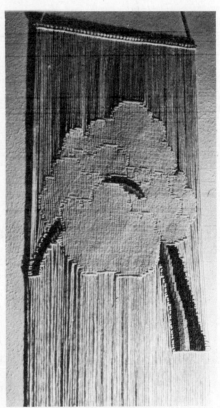

"Allaciare" *displays solidly interwoven color areas, one method of moving color successfully through a macramé piece. Design: Marion Ferri.*

"Lighter than air" look *is achieved here by designing with the fluid draping quality of the cord in mind rather than the knots themselves. Design: Estelle Carlson.*

Texture and color movement *are heightened by combining Cavandoli knotting with a flat linear background in this hanging. Design: Jane Dodge.*

Macramé Projects: A Selection

p. 64

p. 54

p. 60

p. 73

p. 52

p. 68

p. 62

Macramé Projects for Everyone

You'll see by previewing some of the projects on the following pages that macramé has many faces. Here are colors and forms to delight the eye, function and versatility to satisfy the mind. Now that you know the basics, try your hand at macramé; but first give some attention to the information given on this page. It will help in your preparations for knotting.

Planning Ahead

Determining the cord lengths you will need for practice and for projects involves a little simple arithmetic. Cord lengths can't be calculated to the inch, for they must take into account your individual knotting style, the material you plan to use, and the pattern you choose. A good rule is to calculate and then add an extra yard or so for error. Suggestions for replacing over-shortened cord appear on pages 26 and 27.

By considering the following questions, you can approximate the length of cord you'll need.

How long is the project? Each cord should be at least four to five times the finished length of the project. However, since each cord is usually doubled when it is mounted on the heading piece (such as a buckle or frame), it should be cut eight to ten times the length of the finished project.

Is the pattern you've chosen lacy or close? If the pattern is very loose, you may need only six to seven times the finished length.

Is your cord thick or thin? Figure a longer length for thicker cords and a

Once you are acquainted with the basics of macrame, the real fun begins. On the pages that follow are some beautifully designed macrame projects for you to try . . . some decorative, some functional; some easy, some advanced.

You'll find clear instructions and easy-to-follow drawings to make your knotting more enjoyable. Bon appetit!

shorter length for very fine cords.

Will there be many vertical double half hitch knots in the piece? This knot uses up cord very rapidly, so plan accordingly.

Wrapping a Bobbin

Long cord ends have a tendency to tangle and get in the way, and a "butterfly bobbin" is the best method of wrapping up excess cord, avoiding tangles. Start at the free end of the cord and pull it in a figure 8 path around your thumb and index finger. Continue until you have wrapped to about six to eight inches below the mounting knot. Slip the cord off your hand by grasping it in the center of the figure 8. Put a rubber band or twist-tie around the center of the bundle to hold it securely. The bobbin will now feed off cord as you need it during knotting.

Project Directions

To clarify the macramé process, we've devised a simplified knotting and directional code. Instead of spelling out the name of each knot and the direction in which it is angled, we've used abbreviations. A list of the knots and their symbols appears below.

Note: Equipment has not been specified for individual projects. Refer to page 24 for suggested working surfaces for different types of projects. The use of pins and accessories is an individual matter; choose the approach that works for you.

Knotting Key:

ADDHH—Alternate Diagonal Double Half Hitch
AHH—Alternate Half Hitch
ASK—Alternate Square Knot
DHH—Double Half Hitch
HC—Holding Cord
HK—Half Knot
JK—Josephine Knot
LH—Lark's Head

MC—Mounting Cord
MK—Mounting Knot
OK—Overhand Knot
RDHH—Reverse Double Half Hitch
RMK—Reverse Mounting Knot
SK—Square Knot
VDHH—Vertical Double Half Hitch
WC—Working Cord

C—Center
L—Left
R—Right
UC—Upper Center
UL—Upper Left
UR—Upper Right
LC—Lower Center
LL—Lower Left
LR—Lower Right

Openwork Pillow Cover

(Color photo on page 39)

A beautiful accent for any sofa or chair, this macramé-covered pillow in earthy colors is an easy project for beginners.

Materials: Twenty-three 5-yard lengths and one 30-inch length of brown rya rug yarn; six 5-yard lengths of orange rya rug yarn; five 5-yard lengths of black rya rug yarn; ¾ yard of closely woven white wool fabric; white thread; needle.

How to make:

1. Fold the 30-inch length of brown yarn in half to make the MC, and pin 1 of the halves to the working surface with the fold at the R edge and the remainder of the cord hanging free.

2. Mount all cords at their midpoints, repeating the following sequence 5 times from L to R: 2 brown, 1 orange, 2 brown, 1 black; end with 2 brown, 1 orange, 1 brown.

3. Working from the L, knot 1 row of DHH. Follow with 1 row of DHH from R to L. Pin both HC aside.

4. Knot 3 rows of alternating triple SK, concealing the orange and black cords by using them throughout as HC **(fig. 1)**.

5. Knot 5 rows of ASK, allowing the colors to show in every other row, where they are used as WC **(fig. 2)**.

6. Repeat step 4.

7. Repeat step 5.

8. Repeat step 4.

9. Secure the lower edge by knotting 2 rows of DHH, using the far L or R WC for both HC; then OK each WC just below the last row of DHH and cut off extra cord.

10. To make a simple pillow, cut two 13 by 11-inch rectangles of closely woven white wool fabric. Sandwich the macramé cover between the two rectangles, placed with their right sides together. Stretch and pin the macramé piece at all edges until it is evenly held in place. Using a ½-inch seam allowance, sew around 3 sides of the pillow, beginning and ending slightly into the 4th side **(fig. 3)**. Turn the pillow right side out, being sure that the knotted piece is right side up. Stuff the pillow with dacron and slipstitch along the opening to close it **(fig. 4)**.

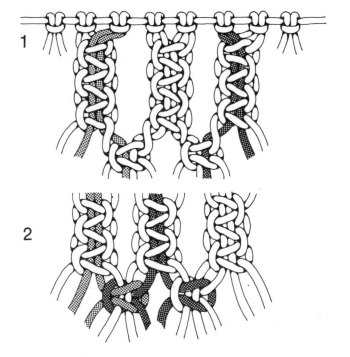

1

2

3

4

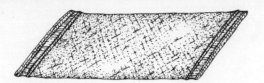

Pretty Placemats

(Color photo on page 39)

Materials: One 30-inch length of royal blue jute; forty-seven 5-yard lengths of royal blue jute; one 10-yard length of royal blue jute; white glue.

How to make:

1. Fold the 30-inch length of jute to make a 15-inch-long double HC; then pin it firmly to the working surface. Mark off into thirteen 1-inch intervals with T-pins, leaving 1 inch free at each end of the double HC **(fig. 1)**.

2. Working from L to R, mount each 5-yard length of jute at its midpoint to the HC.

3. When all 5-yard cords are mounted, fold the 10-yard length of jute into 2 lengths, one of 7 yards and one of 3 yards. Mount this cord at its fold to the HC, following the last MK at the right. The long cord should be placed to fall at the outside R edge.

4. Space the MK as evenly as possible along the HC (for smaller cord more lengths may be needed; add in multiples of 4); then, using the long cord on the R edge as HC, knot a horizontal row of DHH from R to L.

5. Tie 4 rows of VDHH with the long cord as WC and the remaining cords as HC.

6. Knot 1 row of DHH with the long cord as HC.

7. Tie 35 rows of alternating 1½ SK **(fig. 2)**. This section of the project should measure from about 13½ inches to 14 inches in length.

8. Using the long cord on the L edge, knot a row of DHH from L to R.

9. Repeat step 5.

10. Repeat step 6, but knot *single* HH instead of DHH, except for the 1st and the last knots on either edge; these should be individual DHH.

11. Trim off all ends about 1 inch from final row of knots; then glue all ends to the wrong side of the placemat. Allow glue to dry overnight before using.

Richly knotted in royal blue, this smart yet sturdy jute placemat makes a good beginner's project. Only three knots are used: the double half hitch, the vertical double half hitch, and the alternate square knot.

Left Edge

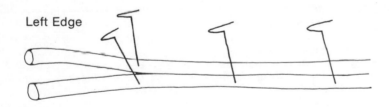

1

Right Edge

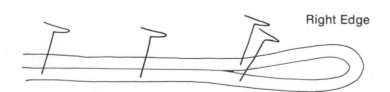

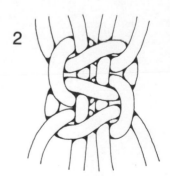

2

For capitalized abbreviations, see Knotting Key on page 35.

Miniature Rainbow Hanging

(Color photo on page 39)

Perle cotton in myriad colors criss-crosses this petite but powerful hanging, making it a perfect means for learning how to move colors in macramé. The design itself is an easy to medium-level challenge using only four knots: the double half hitch, the vertical double half hitch, the half knot chain, and the square knot.

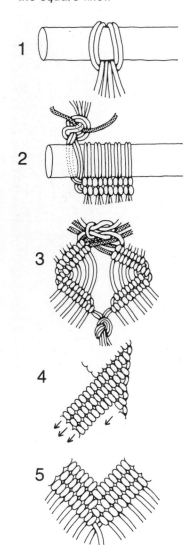

Materials: 90-inch lengths of perle cotton in the following quantities and colors: 6 turquoise, 4 grape, 8 mauve, 4 orange, 8 blue, 4 red, 10 gold, and 4 lime green; twenty-two 18-inch lengths of blue perle cotton; two 15-inch lengths of gold perle cotton; a 4½-inch-long wooden bar, dowel, or other mount.

How to make:

1. Find the midpoints of all cords and mount them *in pairs* with RMK onto the bar **(fig. 1)** in the following order (L to R): 1 grape, 2 mauve, 1 orange, 2 blue, 1 red, 2 gold, 1 lime, 2 turquoise, 1 lime, 2 gold, 1 red, 2 blue, 1 orange, 2 mauve, 1 grape, 1 gold.

2. Center 1 strand of turquoise below the RMK and across the entire width of the piece, leaving an equal length of cord on either side. Using this cord as HC, knot a horizontal row of DHH, using not individual cords but *pairs* of cords as WC.

3. Repeat step 2 with a 2nd strand of turquoise; then at either side, below the bar, cross the ends of both turquoise HC. Next, go above the bar, recross the ends, and tie an OK with both cords to secure. At their midpoints, add in the two 15-inch lengths of gold, 1 at either side **(fig. 2)**.

4. Using pairs of cords as single WC, tie a 2-inch HK sinnet on each edge, using the gold cords as HC.

5. Join the chains with a SK; then, using the individual gold cords as HC and individual turquoise cords as WC, knot a diamond motif as in **figure 3**. Cut off ends 1 inch below diamond.

From this point on, *all* knots are tied using *pairs* of cords as WC and as HC.

6. Using the grape cords at L and the gold cords at R as WC, tie 1-inch HK sinnets over 2 mauve HC at L and 2 grape HC at R.

7. At C, angle last turquoise cord at R of central group from UC to LR. Using cords lime through mauve, knot 8 diagonal decreasing DHH rows, ending with mauve

knots and leaving HC ends free at R.

8. Repeat step 7 for L side, starting with last turquoise cord as first HC and ending with mauve knots.

9. From UR to LRC, knot 11 diagonal rows of VDHH, using all cords from the gold HK sinnet as the first 4 HC; follow with 1 turquoise, 2 lime, 4 gold, and 1 red as HC.

10. Repeat step 9 for L side, working from UL to LLC and using all cords from the mauve HK sinnet as the first 4 HC; follow with 3 turquoise, 2 lime, and 4 gold as HC.

11. At C, group cords red through orange on R and knot a ½-inch HK sinnet, using blue cords as WC and red and orange cords as HC. Repeat for L side, grouping gold through blue cords with blue cords as WC and red and gold cords as HC.

12. Join the blue HK sinnets at C and knot ½ inch of HK sinnet, using 2 blue cords as WC and remaining cords of 1st sinnets as HC.

13. Use HC from last 3 VDHH rows on R as first HC for a series of 8 diagonal DHH rows from UR to LC **(fig. 4)**; follow the mauve knots with cord from the center sinnet in this order: 1 blue, 1 gold, 3 red, 2 blue. Repeat for L side, following orange knots with cords from central sinnet in this order: 2 blue, 1 orange, 2 blue, 1 orange, 1 blue.

14. Divide the HC from the first 5 rows of DHH on either side into 2 equal groups; then tie a SK with the 2 upper groups as HC and the 2 lower groups as WC.

15. Use these cords to complete the last 3 rows of DHH on either side of C, coming to a point at the very center **(fig. 5)**.

16. Group the turquoise and lime cords at the point; then add in two 18-inch blue cords by looping them at their midpoints through the last DHH knot. Tie a ½-inch HK sinnet with the deep blue cords as WC and secure the end of the WC with an OK. Clip WC ends 4½ inches from end of sinnet.

17. Divide cords to R of sinnet into 5 equal groups and repeat step 16 for each group.

18. Repeat step 17 for L side.

A

A. Openwork Pillow Cover, page 36
A latticelike design is produced in this softly muted pillow cover when variations are made on the alternate square knot pattern.
Design: Kathryn Arthurs.

C

C. Miniature Rainbow Hanging, page 38
Colors and curves abound in this pretty little perle cotton wall hanging. Tack it up wherever you want to add a bright spot of color.
Design: Helen Freeman.

B. Pretty Placemats, page 37
Only two knots are needed to make a smart indigo blue placemat in rough jute cord.
Design: Kathryn Arthurs.

B

Eden Pattern Tablerunner

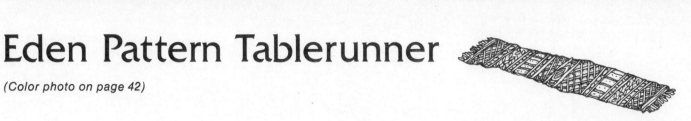

(Color photo on page 42)

Kin to a sampler, this table runner is a versatile project. Instead of leaving it a continuous length, you can cut it into individual place mats. Or create an ornate shawl by doubling the number of cords used.

Materials: Fifty 8-yard lengths of orange 3-ply knitting worsted.

How to make:

1. This project is begun at its center point. Pin the midpoint of each WC to the top of your working surface, hanging one half of each cord behind the board and the other half at the front of the board. Number the cords from L to R; then use the far L WC as HC for 1 row of DHH knotted from L to R.

2. Pattern 1: Using cord 26 as HC, knot a diagonal row of DHH from UC to LL. Follow with a diagonal row of DHH from UC to LR, using cord 25 as HC.

3. Repeat step 2, using cords 24 and 27 instead of cords 25 and 26 as HC.

4. Tie a SK bundle with the C 22 WC; use 3 WC at either side for the WC and the remaining 16 cords as HC **(fig. 1)**.

5. Use WC 38 and 15 as HC for diagonal rows of DHH from UL and UR, crossing, and meeting at LC.

6. Repeat step 5, using WC 39 and 14 as HC for the cross.

7. Tie 2 SK bundles as in step 4, 1 with the L group of WC and 1 with the R group of WC.

8. Complete the diamond-shaped areas in step 7 by first continuing the diagonal rows of DHH begun in steps 5 and 6 from UC to LLC and LRC; then use the HC from the diagonal rows of DHH knotted in steps 2 and 3 as HC to knot diagonal rows of DHH from UL and UR to LLC and LRC, meeting the diagonal rows coming down from UC.

9. Use the far L WC as HC for a row of DHH from L to R.

10. Pattern 2: Count in 8 WC from the L; then use the next 4 WC to knot 2 JK as in **figure 2**. Count over 6 more WC; then use the next 4 WC to knot 2 JK. Repeat for the R side, working inward from the R edge.

11. Repeat step 9.

12. Pattern 3: Divide the WC into 5 equal groups of 10 cords each. Knot each group as in **figure 3** for the 1st row of the pattern. Repeat this sequence 2 more

times to complete the pattern.

13. Repeat steps 9, 10, and 9.

14. Pattern 4: Divide the WC into 5 equal groups of 10 cords each. Use the C 2 WC of each group as HC for diagonal rows of DHH from UC to LL and LR. Repeat 4 times as in **figure 4** to complete the 1st row of this pattern, crossing the last pair of HC before beginning the next pattern row. Repeat 1st row 2 more times to complete the entire pattern.

15. Repeat steps 9, 10, and 9.

16. Pattern 5: Divide the WC into 5 equal groups of 10 cords each. Use the far L WC in each group as HC to knot a slightly upward-curving diagonal row of DHH from UL to LR; follow this row with a 2nd row of DHH knotted in the same manner but with a downward curve **(fig. 5)** to complete the 1st row of the pattern.

17. Use the 6th WC of each group as a HC to knot a slightly upward-curving diagonal row of DHH from UR to LL. Follow this row with a 2nd row of DHH knotted in the same manner but with a downward curve **(fig. 6)** to complete the 2nd row of the pattern.

18. Repeat steps 16 and 17 one more time to complete this pattern.

19. Repeat steps 9, 10, and 9.

20. Pattern 6: Divide the WC into 5 equal groups of 10 cords each. For the 1st row, knot a double-X pattern in each group, using the outside cords of each group as HC as in **figure 7**. Repeat 2 more times to complete this pattern.

21. Knot a row of DHH from L to R, using the far L WC as HC; then knot a row of DHH from R to L, using the same HC. Follow with a final row of DHH knotted from L to R over the same HC.

22. Trim fringe to desired length.

23. Roll up the completed knotting and place it in a plastic bag. Turn the work around and again work through steps 1 through 22 for the 2nd half of the runner. Refer frequently to the completed half to check dimensions, length of rows, and design placement.

To make individual place mats, cut through the center of each repeat of Pattern 2 and trim all fringe to an even length.

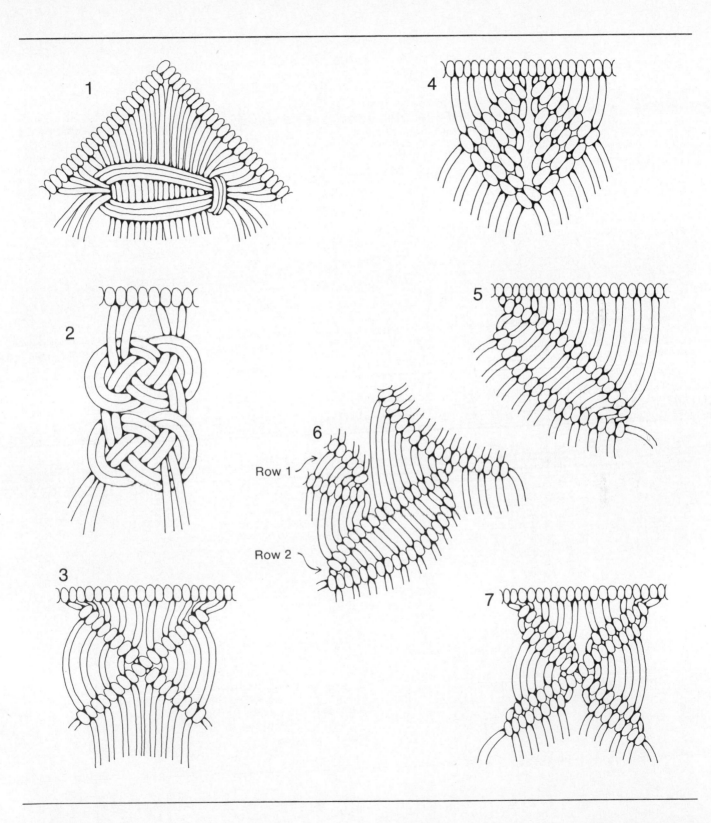

1

2

3

4

5

6
Row 1
Row 2

7

B

A. Outdoor Plant Hanger, page 43

White cotton welting and brown wooden beads combine in a sturdy but attractive plant hanger. A bamboo ring holds up its end beautifully. Design: Kristi Carlson.

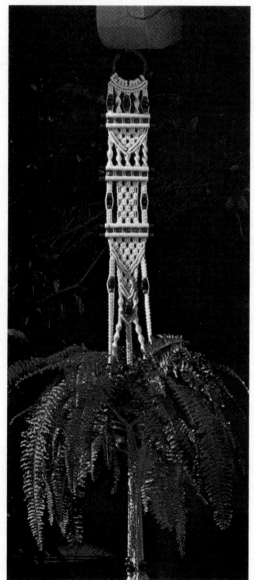

B. Eden Pattern Tablerunner, page 40

Designed to keep table conversation running along complementary lines, this centerpiece is knotted in soft woolen yarn. Overall patterns of leaves and lozenges create a floral motif. Design: Ginger Summit.

A

Outdoor Plant Hanger

(Color photo on page 42)

Materials: Ten 11-yard lengths of ⅛-inch-diameter cotton welting; six 7-inch-long, ⅜-inch-diameter, walnut-stained wooden dowels; one 4½-inch-diameter bamboo or wooden ring; one 2½-inch-diameter brass ring; forty-one 14 mm light brown wooden beads and thirteen 24 mm dark brown wooden beads, each with a large hole.

How to make:

1. Mount the midpoints of all 10 cords to the bamboo ring with MK to make 20 WC.

2. Using the far L cord as HC, tie 1 row of DHH from L to R, curved to follow the ring. Using the same HC, knot 1 curved row of DHH from R to L.

3. Divide the WC into 5 equal groups. Knot 3 SK in groups 1 and 5, and 1 SK in group 3. Onto the 2 HC in each of these 3 groups, thread 1 light brown (hereafter referred to as "LB") bead, 1 dark brown (hereafter referred to as "DB") bead, and 1 LB. Knot 1 SK below each bead group.

4. In groups 2 and 4, knot sinnets of 15 HK each.

5. Knot a row of DHH tightly over one 7-inch dowel.

6. String 1 LB over each of the following cord pairs (L to R): 2, 3; 6, 7; 10, 11; 14, 15; 18, 19.

7. Repeat step 5.

8. Pin the 2 far L and the 2 far R WC aside and then divide the remaining WC into 4 equal groups. Knot 4 decreasing rows of double SK, ending with 1 double SK at C **(fig. 1)**. Use the 2 far L and the 2 far R WC to knot 2 diagonal rows of DHH from UL and from UR to LC **(fig. 2)**.

9. Divide the WC into 5 equal groups and knot each group into HK chains. Groups 1 and 5 have 17 HK; groups 2 and 4 have 11 HK; group 3 has 7 HK.

10. Repeat steps 5 through 7.

11. Divide the WC into 5 equal groups. Knot chains of 4 SK each with groups 1 and 5; then thread 1 LB, 1 DB, 1 LB on the 2 HC and follow with 4½ SK.

12. With the remaining WC groups, knot 7 rows of alternating double SK.

13. Repeat steps 5 through 7.

14. Divide the WC into 5 equal groups. Knot 2 SK in each group.

15. Repeat step 8.

16. Divide the WC into 5 equal groups. In groups 1 and 5, knot chains of 6 SK each; then thread 1 LB, 1 DB, and 1 LB onto the HC of each group. Follow with 33 SK in each chain.

17. Knot 3 SK in groups 2 and 4, and 1 SK in group 3. Pin aside 2 WC on the far L and 2 WC on the far R; then redivide the WC into 2 equal groups and knot 2 double SK in each group. Again, drop 2 WC at each side and knot 1 double SK at C with the remaining 4 WC.

18. Knot 2 diagonal rows of DHH from UL and from UR to LC.

19. Divide the WC into 3 equal groups and knot 11 HK in groups 1 and 3.

20. Tie 1 SK in group 2; then add 1 LB, 1 DB, and 1 LB over the HC. Follow with 1 SK.

21. Knot 1 diagonal row of DHH from UL and from UR to LC.

22. Divide WC into 3 equal groups and knot 58 HK in group 1 and group 3. Knot 24 SK in group 2. All chains should end at the same point.

23. Divide each chain into 2 pairs of WC. Measure 4 inches from the chain ends and knot a circle of double SK using pairs of WC from adjacent chains **(fig. 3)**.

24. About 4 inches below this point, attach the WC with DHH to the brass ring.

25. Divide the cords into 5 equal groups and knot 5 rows of alternating double SK rings, forming a tube. To do this, knot double SK in each of the 5 groups; then divide each group into 2 pairs. Take 1 pair from 1 group and 1 pair from an adjacent group and knot them into double SK. This will start a 2nd ring of knots alternating with the 1st ring. Complete the 2nd ring; then knot rings 3, 4, and 5 in a similar manner.

26. Cut all cords approximately 14 inches below the last row of double SK. Divide the remaining beads into 5 groups, each with 1 DB and 2 LB. OK the beads onto 5 ends; OK the remaining ends, leaving 2 inches free.

Soft cotton welting cord and large wooden beads team up for a plant hanger with the look of outdoors. To protect the cotton from dampness and rot, avoid unglazed pots with drainage holes and locate this hanger in a dry, protected area.

1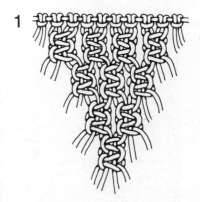

2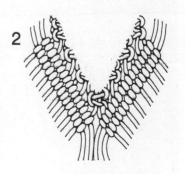

3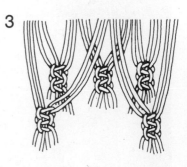

Borromini Hanging

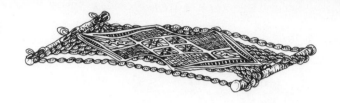

(Color photo on page 47)

If you're an advanced knotter, consider an exercise in sculptural form. This intricately curving wall hanging will be a fitting reward for your investment of time and patience.

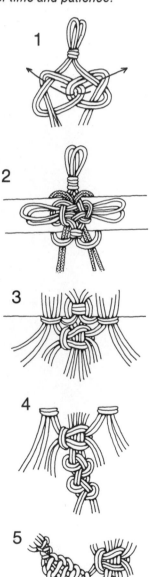

Materials: Eighty 12-yard lengths of #4 Venetian blind cord; two 1⅜-inch-diameter closet dowels, each 2 feet long; 4 wooden drawer pulls whose bases measure 1⅜ inches; 4 ping-pong balls; epoxy glue; white acrylic paint; small paint brush.

How to make:

1. Paint dowels and knobs white and allow to dry overnight.

2. At their midpoints, mount all but 6 cord lengths *in pairs* with MK to make 148 WC. Use the remaining 6 cords to form 3 decorative picot headings.

3. Form 1 picot by folding 2 cords at their midpoints and tying both into 1 OK. As in figure 1, interlock the 2 WC pairs thus formed. To make the large side loops, pull on the C part of the knot (as in **figure 1**) until the entire knot is tight. Secure the picot by knotting a final OK with all 4 WC knotted as 1 cord.

4. Repeat step 3 two more times.

5. Attach each picot to the dowel as shown in **figure 2**. Position 1 picot at a point 1 inch in from *each* dowel end; attach the remaining picot at the very C of the dowel with 78 WC to either side. Use 1 WC pair at either side of this picot to tie a SK over the 4 WC coming from the picot **(fig. 3)**. 5. Knot two 16-inch-long HK sinnets, 1 at far L and 1 at far R, using 12 WC as HC and 4 cords *in pairs* as WC. Set these 2 sinnets aside until step 11.

6. From the C picot, knot a 10½-inch AHH chain, using the 4 WC *in pairs* **(fig. 4)**.

7. Except for the AHH chain in step 6 and the 2 WC immediately at L and at R of this chain, divide the remaining WC into 30 groups of 4 WC each (15 groups on either side of the AHH chain). Starting at the far L, knot 8 inches of HK sinnet; then pull the sinnet over to the C and, using the pair of WC coming out of the SK at C as HC, start to tie individual DHH over the *pair* of HC **(fig. 5)**. Continue to knot HK sinnets and to bring them over to the pair of HC gradually to knot a diagonal row of DHH from UC to LL.

Knot sinnets 2 through 15 in the following lengths: 7 inches, 6 inches, 5 inches, 6 inches, 7 inches, 8 inches, 9 inches, 10 inches, 11 inches, 12 inches, 13 inches, 14 inches, 15 inches, 16 inches, and attach each completed sinnet immediately to the HC.

When the L side is completed, repeat this procedure on the R side, starting with the WC on the far R and numbering inward to C.

8. Knot another pair of diagonal rows of DHH, 1 row from UC to LL, the other from UC to LR, exactly like the previous rows. Use the 1st 2 WC at C on each side as 1 HC **(fig. 6)**.

9. Knot another pair as in step 8, but use only 1 cord from UC as HC in each case. Curve this row slightly downward; then at the end, line it up with previous rows.

10. Using the 1st 20 WC from UC to LL as WC and the 21st WC as HC, knot a diagonal row of DHH from UL to LC, *starting at far L with WC 1* and ending at LC with WC 20. Repeat on R side.

11. Join the main body of the hanging to the large HK sinnet at far L by first knotting a chain of 12 AHH with the HC pairs from the 1st and the 2nd diagonal DHH rows as WC; then divide the 16 WC from the large sinnet into 8 pairs and knot pairs 2, 3, 4, 6, 7, and 8 into chains of 7 AHH each. Knot 2 AHH in chains 1 and 5; then pass the AHH chain from the main body *between* the 2 WC of chains 1 and 5 and secure it in place by OK both chains below the opening thus formed **(fig. 7)**.

Push 1 ping-pong ball up inside of the AHH chains from the large sinnet and tighten the AHH chain from the main body around the ball. Secure this chain by using each of its 4 WC to knot a DHH over the HC of the 3rd diagonal row of DHH in the main body. Regroup all cords from the original large HK sinnet to knot another sinnet of 24 HK. Repeat for the R side.

12. Divide all WC at UC on the L side of the hanging into 5 equal groups of 4 WC. Also divide all WC coming in from the L side into 9 equal groups of 4 WC; the 10th group falls at the LL and has only 3 WC, since the last 2 cords will be used later as HC. Interweave each group as 1 **(fig. 8)**, working from top to bottom. Repeat for R side.

13. Using 2 of the 4 WC from the C AHH chain (see step 6) as 1 HC, knot a diagonal row of DHH from UC to LLC, using all woven cords as WC. Repeat for R side.

14. Using the 1st 14 WC on each side (28 cords in all) as HC, tie a large SK bundle at C with cords 15 through 20 as WC.

15. Knot a slightly curving diagonal row of DHH from UL to LC, using WC 21 as HC. Repeat for R side and join this HC with the HC from the L diagonal row at C when both rows are completed.

16. Using the last 2 cords remaining at far L in step 12 as 1 HC, knot a diagonal row of DHH from UL to LLC, linking with the diagonal row of DHH from UC to LLC in step 13 **(fig. 9)**. Repeat for R side.

17. Divide the 20 WC used for the DHH row in step 16 into 5 equal groups of 4 WC each and knot each group into a sinnet of 24 HK. Repeat for R side.

18. Continue to use the double HC from step 16 as HC for a row of DHH from ULC to LL. Take the WC from the sinnets tied in step 17, working first with the far L sinnet and knotting from ULC to LL.

19. Repeat step 11 for both sides, but follow each with a sinnet of 35 HK.

20. At CL (center left) of the hanging, make 1 more large SK bundle. Use 24 cords as HC (12 from UL and 12 from UC) and 6 cords from each side as WC. Repeat for R side.

21. Continue the crossed diagonal rows of DHH in step 15, working from UC to LLC and LRC; use *all* cords from the SK bundles as WC for each row.

22. Repeat step 20 at C instead of CL.

23. Knot a diagonal row of DHH from UL to LC, starting from the point illustrated in figure 9. Repeat for R side. When both rows are completed, join them at C **(fig. 10)** and use the 4 HC from these 2 rows to knot a chain of 22 AHH at C.

24. Repeat step 12, changing "UC" to read "UL"; also change "in from the side" to read "in from C" and "LL" to read "LC."

25. Using the cords from the woven areas as WC and the 2 centermost cords as HC, knot diagonal rows of DHH, 1 from UC to LLC and 1 from UC to LRC.

26. From UL to LC, knot 1 slightly inward curving diagonal row of DHH over a single HC, incorporating the HC from step

25 as a WC. Knot in reverse order the last 21 WC to be DHH over this HC—that is, start with the top cord and work downward from there. The last WC to be knotted in is the cord closest to the curving diagonal row of DHH. Repeat for R side.

27. Knot 2 more diagonal rows of DHH from UL to LC, using a double HC for the 1st row and a single HC for the 2nd row. Repeat for R side. Use the HC from the last L and R diagonal rows of DHH to knot a SK over the 4 WC from the C AHH chain.

28. Divide the WC into 15 equal groups of 4 WC each and knot HK sinnets in each group. Use the sinnet lengths listed in step 7, working backward from 17 inches to 7 inches. Start at the far L edges and knot the sinnets from UL to LC.

29. To attach all ends to the bottom dowel, start at C and work outward to L edge. Loop *pairs* of cords from back to front around the dowel; then pass them around themselves and knot them into a SK on the wrong side of the hanging **(fig. 11)**. Start with the C AHH chain; then tie on the 2 WC from the C SK.

The next cords to be tied on at C should come from the 1st HK sinnet at far L. Tie on sinnets 2 through 15 in numerical order but tie on from C to *far L* edge. This creates a thick, curved area of sinnets. Repeat for R side.

30. Divide the 8 longest HC from the large HK sinnet at far L into 2 equal groups and knot 1 sinnet of 45 HK with each group. Divide the remaining 8 cords into 2 equal groups and knot 1 sinnet of 3 HK in each group. Attach the cords from these last 2 sinnets to the dowel as in step 29. Loop the remaining 2 cords from front to C back of the dowel, attaching them to previously tied SK. Repeat for R side.

31. Cut cord ends to 1 inch. Secure all knots behind the dowel with epoxy.

32. Attach wooden knobs to all 4 dowel ends with epoxy and allow to dry overnight.

33. To make 1 hanger loop, fold a 2-yard length of cord in half and OK it 2 inches from the fold. Knot a chain of AHH as long as you desire. Repeat for 2nd hanger loop. Tie hangers to upper dowel with SK and secure the knots with epoxy.

6

7

8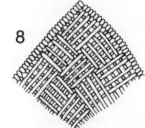

9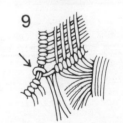

10

11 SK View From Back of Dowel
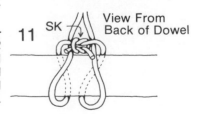

Pagoda Bell Chimes

(Color photo on page 47)

The unique appearance of these wind chimes is due to their spiraling three-dimensional bell cords. The simple technique used here is explained in detail on page 16.

Materials: Six 10-yard lengths of gold or blue jute cord; one oval-shaped iron link or equivalent; one large beaten brass bell or cow bell; white glue.

How to make:

1. Group all 6 WC together at their midpoints. One inch away from the midpoint, at each side, knot two 7-inch-long sinnets of HK, using the two outside cords in each group as WC and the remainder as HC **(fig. 1)**. Be sure to knot both sinnets to twist in the same direction.

2. When the sinnets are completed, slip the link onto the sinnets and hold it at the 2-inch unknotted section between sinnets while you twist them together to form a tubelike shape **(fig. 2)**.

3. To begin the larger spiral section, knot 11 decreasing rows of DHH from R to L, using the far R WC as the first HC and working downward from there **(fig. 3)**.

4. Upon completion of this 1st triangular shape, turn and repin your work so that the WC hang downward. Again start from the right as in step 3 and knot a triangle of 11 decreasing rows of DHH.

5. Repeat step 4 seven more times, turning your work as you progress, for a total of 9 spiraling triangles, each with 11 rows.

6. From this point on, the number of rows in the triangles will decrease: triangle 10 will have only 10 rows; triangles 11 through 16, 9 rows each; triangles 17 and 18, 8 rows each; and triangles 19 and 20, 7 decreasing rows each. Follow triangle 20 with a single row of DHH from R to L to secure all WC. To delete extra cords, knot the first rows of triangles 10, 11, 17, and 19 over 2 HC from the far R edge. Two-thirds into the row, cut off the extra cord and complete the row of DHH **(fig. 4)**.

7. Using the 2 outside cords as WC and the remaining cords as HC, knot 3 SK, each separated by a 1-inch interval. Loop the 8 cords through the bell ring and double them back on themselves 4 inches down from the last SK. Working up from the bell ring, knot enough SK over all WC to reach the last SK. Clip excess cord and glue the knot.

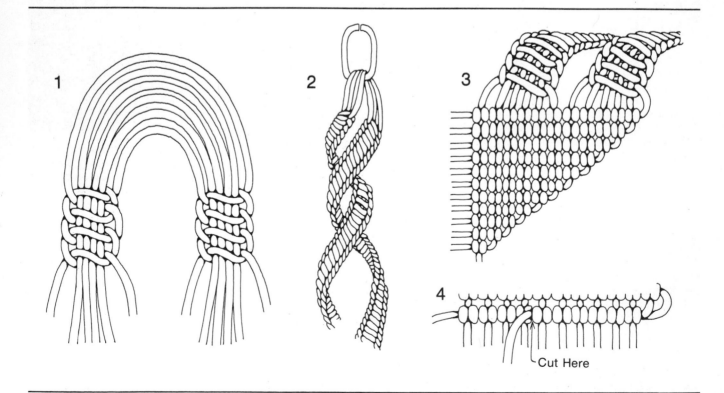

1

2

3

4

Cut Here

A. Borromini Hanging, page 44

Inspired by the unusual structural designs of a 17th century Italian Baroque architect, this unique knotted and plaited hanging of cotton clothesline cord flows into soft, three-dimensional surfaces based on geometric relationships. Design: Gertrude Reagan.

B. Pagoda Bell Chimes, page 46

Reminiscent of tier-roofed Japanese temples, these spiraling bell chimes will hold small hanging plants if extra cord is added. Design: Sandra Cummings.

Mexican Olé Rebozo

(Color photo on page 50)

Wrap yourself in color when you wear this Mexico-inspired rebozo. Its loose, open macramé pattern makes it an ideal shawl for cool summer evenings. If you'd like something with more density, knot only horizontal rows of double half hitches set more closely together. This means that you'll need a holding cord at least three times longer than the length indicated at right.

Materials: 7-yard lengths of 3-ply rope-like wool yarn in the following amounts and colors: 6 lengths of blue green, 10 of light blue, 10 of royal purple, 10 of lemon yellow, 20 of red orange; one 21-yard length of red orange, 3-ply, ropelike wool yarn.

How to make:

1. Using a 36-inch square of fiberboard as your working surface, pin the midpoint of each cord to the top edge of the board in this order (L to R): 4 light blue, 8 red orange, 2 blue green, 2 lemon yellow, 2 royal purple, 2 light blue, 2 lemon yellow, 4 red orange, 2 lemon yellow, 2 blue green, 2 royal purple, 2 light blue, 2 royal purple, 6 red orange, 2 lemon yellow, 4 royal purple, 2 light blue, 2 blue green, 2 lemon yellow, 2 red orange.

Half of each length should fall behind the board, and half should fall to the front of the board. Bundle the cords that are behind the board into a paper bag to keep them out of your way while you work.

2. Find the midpoint of the 21-yard-long red cord and pin it at C of the top of the fiberboard square. This cord will be used strictly as a HC, the only one used throughout the project. All other cords will be used only as WC.

3. Knot a horizontal row of DHH from R to L over the red HC. Move the R half of this long cord to the back of the board and enclose it in the bag with the other extra cord lengths. It will be used for the 2nd half of the shawl. From this point on, use only the L cord end for this half of the shawl.

4. At a point 5 inches below the 1st row of DHH, knot a 2nd horizontal row of DHH from L to R.

5. Knot a row of 3½ deep Vs from R to L; each side of 1 V should have 8 WC (16 WC for each V), and the bottom of the V should fall at a point 5 inches below the last horizontal DHH row **(fig. 1)**.

6. From L to R, knot a row of 3½ shallow Vs, following the procedure outlined in step 5. This row of Vs should meet the previous row of Vs to make a row of open diamonds, as in **figure 2**.

7. Knot a row of 3½ shallow Vs from R to L to meet the previous row of Vs in a way that produces broad, open diamonds **(fig. 3)**. Each side of 1 V should have 8 WC (16 WC for each V).

8. Repeat step 5 but work from L to R. The bottom of each deep V should fall at a point 7 inches below the top of each shallow V in the previous row **(fig. 4)**.

9. Knot a horizontal row of DHH from R to L, directly below the bottoms of the deep Vs in the last row.

10. Five inches below the horizontal row of DHH in step 9, knot 3 horizontal rows of DHH.

11. Follow this horizontal row of DHH with 3½ shallow Vs knotted from R to L. The bottom of each V should fall 3 inches below the horizontal row **(fig. 5)**.

12. Divide the WC into 14 groups of 4 WC each; include the red HC in the far L 4-cord group to make a bundle of 5 cords.

13. OK each bundle as though it were 1 cord at a point 4 to 5 inches below the last row of shallow Vs. Redivide the WC into new groups of 4 cords each by taking 2 cords from each adjacent OK and making a new, alternate bundle **(fig. 6)**.

14. Knot a total of 5 rows of alternate OK to end the shawl.

15. Cut all cord ends to 10 inches; then carefully unravel each 3-ply cord into its separate plies to fringe the shawl.

16. For the 2nd half of the shawl, repeat steps 4 through 14.

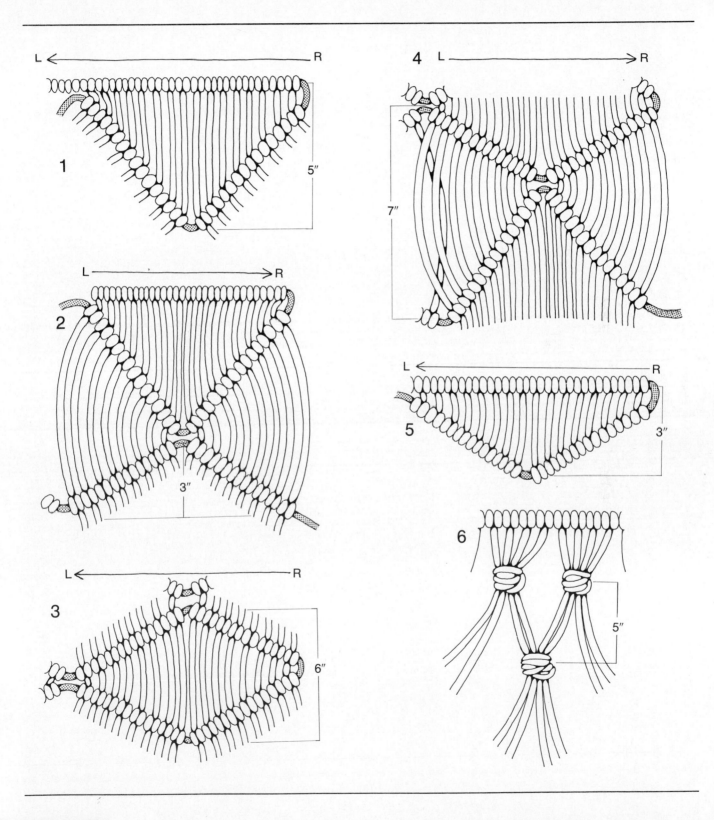

A. Artful Apothecary Jar, page 51
Give instant interest to your kitchen by covering an apothecary jar with openwork macramé. Design: Ginger Summit.

A

B. Mexican Olé Rebozo, page 48
Earthy, primitive colors flow across this dramatic fringed rebozo. Based on a traditional Mexican macramé technique, this variation uses ropelike, woolen yarns. Design: Alyson Smith Gonsalves.

B

Artful Apothecary Jar

(Color photo on page 50)

Materials: Apothecary jar 9½ inches tall by 4½ inches square (with cap); thirty-two 6-foot lengths, fifteen 24-inch lengths, and one 1-yard length of ⅛-inch braided nylon cord; white glue.

How to make:

1. RMK 25 cords at their midpoints at a point equidistant from both ends of one 6-yard length of cord (used here as both a MC and a WC). To form a large circle, RMK the remaining 7 cords at their midpoints over *both* ends of the HC **(fig. 1)**. Drape the MC around the neck of the jar and pull on both ends of the MC to cinch the cords up around the neck.

2. Knot 3 rounds of ASK around the entire jar to cover the neck.

3. Divide the 64 WC into 4 equal groups, each arranged to correspond to one flat side of the jar. Work a side at a time.

4. Number the 16 WC from L to R. Using WC 8 and 9 as HC, knot 2 SK with WC 7 and 10; set them aside. Continue to knot SK in this manner, using the following cord pairs as WC: 6 and 11, 5 and 12, 4 and 13, 3 and 14, 2 and 15, 1 and 16. Set each WC pair aside after its SK is tied.

5. For the 2nd half of the design, set aside WC 1 and 16. Start tying single SK, using the following cord pairs in this order: 2 and 15, 3 and 14, 4 and 13, 5 and 12, 6 and 11, 7 and 10. Allow the loose cords to form a soft, oval shape between the upper and the lower design areas (see photo on page 50).

6. To complete the design, knot 3 rows of ASK, starting with the C 12 WC in the 1st row and increasing to include all 16 WC in the 2nd row. Follow with a 3rd row of 3 ASK.

7. Repeat steps 4 through 6 three more times, once for each side of the jar.

8. When all 4 sides are completed, turn the jar upside down and join all WC into 1 continuous round of SK.

9. To cover the jar bottom, knot successive rows of ASK, pushing the knots against the bottom as you work.

10. As rounds become smaller, cut WC ends to 1 inch but *only* after they have been used as HC for an ASK. Tuck these cord ends under the previously knotted portion. Continue in this manner until the entire bottom is covered.

11. To cover the jar cap, fold one 24-inch-long cord in half and fold the 1-yard-long piece at a point 12 inches from one end. Pin folds next to each other on a piece of fiberboard. Tie a SK as in **figure 2**. Repeat 3 more times to form 4 individual SK.

12. Pin these 4 SK in a circle, with knots at C and WC radiating outward. Join the 4 SK by using 1 WC from each of 2 adjacent SK as HC and using a *new* WC at its midpoint to tie a SK **(fig. 3)**. Join all SK in this manner to form a round of 8 SK chains. Knot 4 SK in each of the 4 original SK chains and 3 SK in each of the secondary SK chains. If needed, add extra SK to each chain to cover the cap to its lip. Remove cords from fiberboard and place over jar cap.

13. To secure knotting to jar cap, use longest WC as HC for a round of DHH snugly fitting base of cap. Pull on HC to tighten the fit. Follow with a 2nd row of DHH knotted over the same HC.

14. Tuck the end of the HC firmly under the knotting; then clip all cords as close to the last DHH round as possible. To secure the cut cord ends, apply white glue below the last DHH row all around the cap.

Here's a decorative idea that's quick and relatively easy: a large apothecary jar is covered with lacelike openwork macramé in braided nylon cord. The covered jar is especially attractive when filled with brightly colored candies or dried fruit.

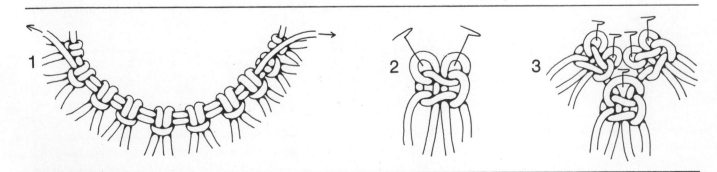

Starburst Necklace

(Color photo on page 55)

Design elements separated by square knot chains give this necklace an air of sophisticated simplicity. Begun from the clasp, the neck strands are joined at the bottom into a single diamond-shaped pendant with half hitch spirals for fringe. This is an intermediate-to-advanced project.

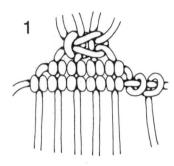

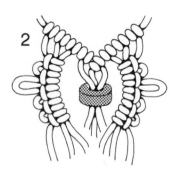

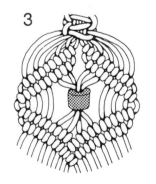

Materials: Eighteen 3-yard lengths and one 48-inch length of beige #18 waxed nylon cord; one 48-inch length of chocolate brown #18 waxed nylon cord; 18 small copal blue glass beads; 16 medium copal and light blue striped barrel beads; 6 small brown beads; 3 large brass beads; 1 clasp; 2 jump rings; white glue.

How to make:

1. Pin the midpoints of two 3-yard lengths of beige cord to the working surface; then, starting ½ inch down from the pin, knot 35 SK. Secure the 1st SK with white glue.

2. Add in WC 3 and 4 as shown in **figure 1.** Thread 1 small blue bead onto the C 2 WC; then knot 2 diagonal rows of DHH from UL and UR to LC below the bead, joining the rows at C.

3. Slide a small brown bead onto the C 2 WC. With the remaining WC, knot 1 chain of 5 LH on either side of the bead, leaving a large loop following knot 2 **(fig. 2).**

4. Use 1 far L and 1 far R WC to knot 8 SK, using remaining WC as HC.

5. Attach WC 5 and 6 as in step 2.

6. Thread a medium blue bead over the C 4 WC; then knot 1 chain of 8 LH on either side of the bead, leaving large loops following knot 2 and knot 5 on each side.

7. Repeat step 4.

8. Using the C 2 WC as HC, knot 1 diagonal row of DHH from UC to LL and to LR. Repeat. Thread a small blue bead onto the C 4 WC; then knot 2 diagonal rows of DHH from UL and from UR to LC **(fig. 3).**

9. Thread a medium blue bead over C 4 WC and knot 1 chain of 11 LH on either side of the bead, leaving large loops following knots 2, 5, and 8 **(fig. 4).**

10. Repeat step 4.

11. Slide a small blue bead over the C 4 WC; then knot 1 chain of 5 LH on either side of the bead, leaving a large loop following knot 2 on each side. Thread 1 small blue bead onto all cords of each LH chain.

12. Using the C 2 WC as HC, knot 1 diagonal row of DHH from UC to LL and to LR; repeat. Follow with a 5-strand Berry Pattern (see page 20), leaving free the L and R HC from the last diagonal DHH rows. When the Berry Pattern is completed, use the free L and R HC to curve single rows of DHH around the berry, leaving the HC uncrossed at the end. With the outermost WC on each side as HC, knot a second curving row of DHH from UL and from UR to LC, crossing them at the end **(fig. 5).**

13. Knot 1 chain of 8 LH on either side with the 2 far L and the 2 far R WC, leaving large loops after knots 2 and 5; then knot 1 chain of 3 LH with the next 2 WC on either side. Leave the last 2 WC free.

14. Repeat step 12, continuing to use the 2 crossed C cords as HC and starting to knot with the 2 free WC in step 12. Divide the WC into 3 equal groups and thread 1 small blue bead onto each group. Knot 1 chain of 8 LH with the L group and with the R group, leaving large loops after knots 2 and 5 on each side.

15. Repeat step 4.

16. Slide 1 large brass bead over the C 4 WC; then knot 1 chain of 11 LH at L and at R, leaving large loops after knots 2, 5, and 8.

17. Repeat step 4.

18. Repeat step 8, but use 1 barrel bead.

19. Repeat step 13.

20. Repeat step 8, but use 1 barrel bead.

21. Knot 1 chain of 8 LH with the 4 WC at L, leaving large loops following knots 2 and 5. Knot 3 SK with the C 4 WC; then knot 5 LH with the R 4 WC.

22. Repeat steps 1 through 21 for the 2nd neck strand, reversing order of chains.

23. Thread both beige and brown 48-inch lengths through 1 small brown bead and position the bead at the midpoints of the cords. Pin the bead and cords to the working surface with the beige color above the chocolate color; then pin the ends of both finished strands adjacent to the bead and cords in a slight (15°) diagonal position **(fig. 6).**

24. Using the beige cord as HC on both sides, knot 1 slightly diagonal row of DHH from UC to LL and to LR, using the cords from both strands as WC.

25. Knot 1 diagonal row of VDHH directly under the previous row of DHH, using the chocolate cord as WC and working outward from UC to LL and to LR.

26. Using the C 2 WC as HC, knot 1 slightly diagonal row of DHH from UC to LL and to LR.

27. Thread 1 small brown bead onto both the beige and the chocolate HC at both outside edges.

28. Thread 1 large brass bead onto the C 4 WC. Knot 1 chain of 10 LH with the adjacent 2 WC at either side of the brass bead.

29. Thread 1 small blue bead over the next 4 WC at either side. Knot 2 LH with the next 2 WC at each side. Leave the last outer WC free.

30. Repeat step 26, but work from UL and UR to LC, using the HC from the last diagonal row of DHH **as** HC.

31. Repeat step 25, working inward from UL and UR to LC.

32. Repeat step 24, working from UL and UR to LC. Complete the diamond shape as in **figure 7**, passing the chocolate and the beige HC from the L and from the R through a brown bead at the center.

33. Divide the WC into 8 groups, 3 WC in the 2 outside groups at either side and 4 in the remaining 2 groups at either side. The chocolate and beige HC should finish in the 2 groups immediately adjacent to the C brown bead.

34. Using the longest beige cord as WC and the remaining cords as HC, knot 1 chain of HH spirals **(fig. 8)** measuring 1¾ inches long with each of the 2 groups adjacent to the C bead. Working outward from this point, knot at each side 1 HH spiral measuring 1½ inches in length.

35. Knot the next 2 groups of 3 WC into single HH spirals, each 1¼ inches long. The last 2 outside groups of 3 WC are knotted into 1-inch-long HH spirals.

36. Thread 1 medium blue barrel bead onto all cords of each chain and knot all cords in each group as 1 into an OK below each bead. Cut off excess cord and dip knots in white glue to hold.

37. Attach jump rings and clasp to loops at ends of necklace strands.

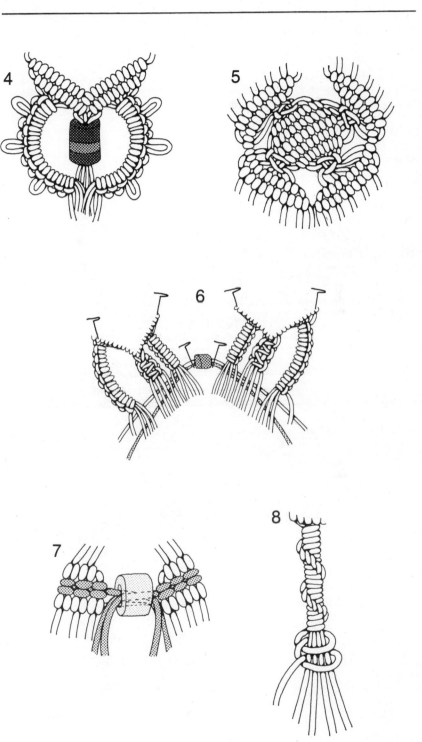

4

5

6

7

8

Hopi-Style Rope Basket

(Color photo on page 55)

Macramé doesn't have to be limited to two dimensions—sculptural pieces like this coiled basket are surprisingly easy to construct. Double half hitches are knotted over an outwardly spiraling rope core to hold the basket together, while secondary colors are added as the basket expands.

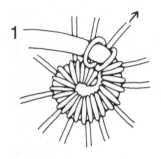

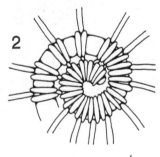

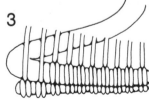

Basket Lip

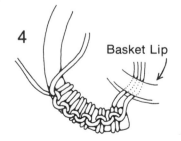

Materials: One 50-foot length of ¼-inch-diameter sisal rope; 304 yards of white 18-thread cotton cable cord; 40 yards of maroon 18-thread cotton cable cord; 30 yards of orange 18-thread cotton cable cord; 20 yards of yellow 18-thread cotton cable cord; crochet hook; white glue.

How to make:

1. Taper off 1 end of the rope by cutting it at a slant.

2. Cut the white cotton cord into 4-yard lengths and, with RMK, attach 12 lengths at their midpoints to the tapered end of the rope core.

3. Force the knot-covered tapered end into a very tight circle, approximately 1 inch across, and secure the circle by knotting a DHH over the core with the first WC that was mounted on the core **(fig. 1)**.

4. To continue the flat outward spiral of the core, use the mounted WC to join the next round of rope to the previous round with continuous DHH **(fig. 2)**. Work the knots as tightly as possible, keeping the rounds moving outward on a flat plane.

5. As areas open up on the core between the WC, attach new WC as in step 2 and use them just as the original WC are used. Continue to add cords as needed until the shape of the basket begins to taper inward.

6. After 6 complete rounds have been knotted, gradually adjust the core to lie slightly above the previous round **(fig. 3)**. Continue this method for 2 more rounds, gradually expanding the basket as you go.

7. At the 3rd round, introduce the pattern by cutting an 8-yard length of maroon cord and looping it at its midpoint over the core of the basket. Continue to work rounds until the opposite side of the basket is reached; then position a 2nd 4-yard maroon cord over the rope directly opposite the first maroon cord.

8. Continue to coil and knot the core to a point 2½ inches before the original

maroon cord; then attach a 3rd maroon cord as in step 7. When the original maroon cord is reached, knot a single DHH with one maroon WC, leaving the 2nd maroon WC unused. Follow this with a 4th maroon WC added at a point 2½ inches past the maroon DHH.

9. Repeat step 8 for the opposite design.

10. Continue to work upward on the basket, adding in orange and yellow cords to colored designs where needed (see photo on page 55).

11. Begin to decrease the diameter of the basket and to taper the designs back in the 11th row up from the bottom of the basket. To delete cords, work them to the inside of the basket, leaving about 2 inches hanging free and cutting off any remaining cord.

12. From row 17 onward, work the rounds into a cylindrical shape with straight sides. Small color patterns should be completed by row 18, main patterns by row 19.

13. When the last color cord has been deleted, knot 1 more round of DHH to a point falling between the 2 design groups. Cut WC ends and glue to the inside of the basket neck. Leave the core uncut.

14. To make the handles, cut four 2-foot lengths of white cord and insert them from the outside of the basket between rounds 12 and 13, 2 cords at each side of the basket. SK each pair of cords inside the basket and glue them down.

15. Cut two 4-inch lengths of rope and use each of these as a core over which 14 SK are tied, using the glued-in cords as WC **(fig. 4)**.

16. Pass the rope ends and cords between the last 2 coils of the neck and knot into place with the WC. Fringe the ends of the rope at the inside of the basket and cut off the WC.

17. To finish the mouth of the basket, wrap the core with cord for an inch or so; then cut the rope and glue it to the round below, holding the cotton cord to the inside of the basket. When glue is dry, cut off the remaining length of rope.

A. Starburst Necklace, page 52

Staccato starbursts of copal blue and brass beads punctuate this necklace of seemingly intricate, interlocked, Celtic-style motifs made with berry knots and square knot chains. Design: Barbara DeOca.

B. Hopi-style Rope Basket, page 54

Southwestern colors and Indian motifs decorate this jug-shaped basket. Made almost entirely with cotton cord double half hitched over a rope core, it's surprisingly firm. Design: Nilda Duffek.

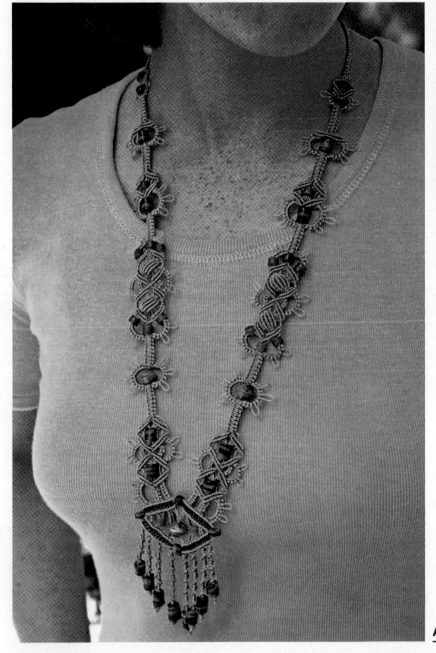

Nubby Textured Rug

(Color photo on page 58)

Think big! Make yourself a beautifully durable macramé rug of heavy jute cord. An intermediate-level project, the rug measures 26 by 44 inches when completed and employs only two knots—the alternate diagonal double half hitch and the double half hitch.

Materials: Fifty-two 32-foot lengths of beige 3-ply heavy jute cord; sixteen 32-foot lengths of brown 7-ply heavy jute cord; sixteen 32-foot lengths of black 7-ply heavy jute cord.

How to make:

1. This project is started in the middle and worked outward to the ends. Pin the midpoint of each cord to the top edge of a 36 by 36-inch square of fiberboard, one half of each cord falling behind the board and one half falling in front of the board, in the following order (L to R): 2 beige. Repeat this sequence 8 times—1 brown, 1 beige. 16 beige. Repeat this sequence 8 times—1 brown, 1 black. 16 beige. Repeat this sequence 8 times—1 beige, 1 black. 2 beige.

2. Knot each of the 2 groups of all beige cords into a decreasing triangle of ADDHH, starting with 8 knots and ending with 1 knot **(fig. 1)**.

3. At L, use beige cords as HC and brown cords as WC to knot 8 increasing diagonal rows of DHH followed by 8 full rows of DHH from UL to LR **(fig. 2)**.

4. Repeat step 3 for the C group of brown and black cords, knotting from UC to LR. Start with black HC and move to beige HC, using brown cords as WC.

5. For 8 diagonal rows of black DHH knotted from UC to LL, use the beige WC from the L ADDHH area as HC.

6. In the far R black cord group, knot 8 increasing diagonal rows of DHH followed by 8 full rows of DHH, using beige as HC and black as WC.

7. Knot 17 *increasing* rows of ADDHH (note in **fig. 3** that each row of knots is repeated once, as: 1st row, 1 knot; 2nd row, 1 knot; 3rd row, 2 knots; 4th row, 2 knots; etc. up to 9 knots on row 17; follow with decreasing rows) at far L and at far R; use beige HC from diagonal brown and black rows at L and at R *plus* 2 beige cords at *each* outside edge as WC. Follow with 16 *decreasing* rows of ADDHH at far L and far R; drop 1 cord from row ends nearest colored WC in each successive row. A triangular area pointing toward C of rug will appear at each edge.

8. At C, knot 15 rows of ADDHH in a diamond shape, using beige HC from C black and brown areas as WC **(fig. 4)**.

9. In L group of brown cords, knot 16 diagonal rows of DHH from UL to LC.

10. In the C group of brown cords, knot 16 more diagonal rows of DHH, followed by 8 diminishing rows of DHH **(fig. 5)** from UL to LR.

11. In the L group of black cords, knot 8 diagonal rows of DHH, followed by 8 diminishing rows of DHH **(fig. 6)** from UC to LL.

12. In C group of black cords, knot 16 diagonal rows of DHH from UC to LL.

13. Knot each group of beige cords at CL and CR, as in step 8.

14. In the L black cord group, knot 8 increasing rows, then 8 full rows of DHH from UL to LLC, using beige cords as HC.

15. Knot 8 diagonal rows of DHH from UC to LL in the C group of black cords, using beige cords as HC.

16. Join both black areas by knotting, in sequence, diminishing chevron-shaped rows, 8 rows on L side, 7 rows on R side, using black for WC and HC **(fig. 7)**.

17. In C group of brown cords, knot 8 diagonal rows of DHH from UC to LR.

18. In the R group of brown cords, knot 8 increasing rows of DHH, followed by 8 full rows of DHH from UR to LC.

19. Join both C and R areas of brown cords by knotting 8 diminishing chevron-shaped rows, using brown for WC and for HC (refer to step 16 and fig. 7).

20. Knot 17 increasing rows of ADDHH (see step 7) in both L and R groups of all beige cords. Follow with 8 decreasing rows of ADDHH and 2 diagonal DHH areas **(fig. 8)**. Use beige cords for all WC.

21. Repeat step 8 at bottom C, referring to figure 4. Knot remaining cords at L and at R of this diamond into 8 diagonal DHH rows at each side (as in fig. 8).

22. Use the far L beige WC as a HC for a horizontal row of DHH from the L to the R edge of the rug.

23. Divide all cords into pairs and OK each pair as 1 cord below the DHH row in step 22. Incorporate the HC in step 22 into the far R OK bundle. Clip all cords to 2 inches.

24. To make the 2nd half of the rug, repeat steps 2 through 24 but change to read "brown" instead of "black" and "black" instead of "brown." The black area will start at L and the brown area will start at R. The only other change will be in step 4—knot the rows of brown from UC to LR.

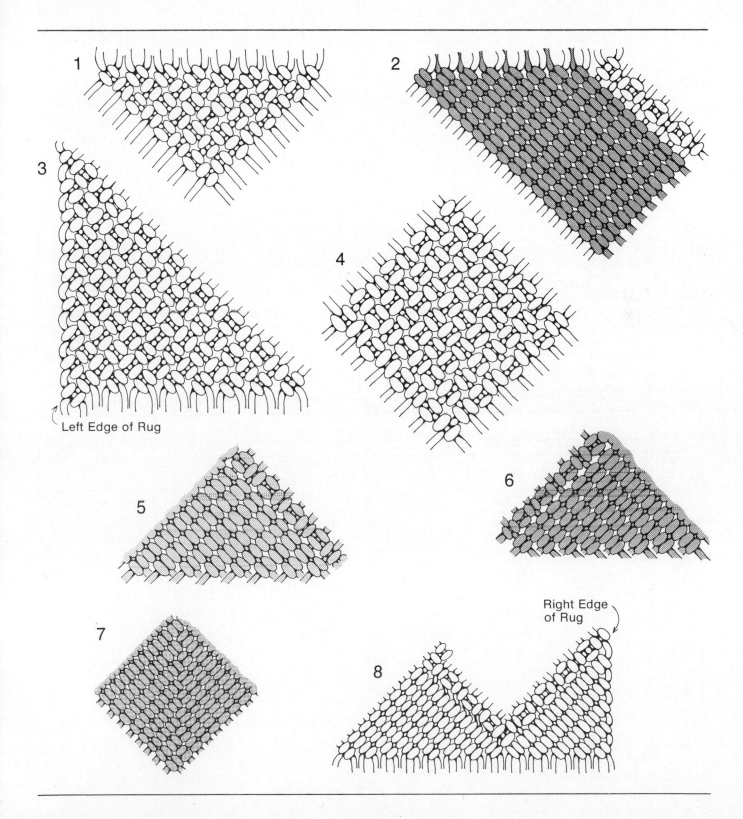

1

2

3

Left Edge of Rug

4

5

6

Right Edge
of Rug

7

8

A. Sculptural Plant Hanger, page 59

Spectacular, with the effect of a carved temple column, this plant hanger of Chinese red jute is an effective foil for your indoor greenery. Design: Joy Coschigano of Hidden House.

B. Nubby Textured Rug, page 56

Bold arrowhead designs are interlocked across the face of this knotted jute rug. Alternate diagonal double half hitches form a seemingly irregular background surface pattern in contrast to the regular ribbing of the two-color, double half hitched arrowheads. Design: Ginger Summit.

A

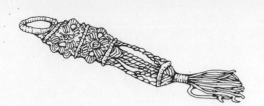

Sculptural Plant Hanger

(Color photo on page 58)

Materials: Six 11-yard lengths, one 4-yard length, two ½-yard lengths, three ¾-yard lengths, and one 3½-yard length of red 5-ply jute cord; six 16-yard lengths and fourteen 1½-yard lengths of orange 5-ply jute cord; two 4-inch-diameter wooden (or metal) rings; six 6½-inch lengths of coat hanger wire; white glue.

How to make:

1. RMK six 16-yard orange cords and six 11-yard red cords to 1 ring in this order: 3 red, 6 orange, 3 red.
2. Wrap the remainder of the ring from L to R with the 4-yard red cord as explained in step 1-A, page 23. When completed, tuck the end through the closest MK on the back; glue and cut excess cord.
3. Using a ½-yard length of red as HC, knot a row of DHH from L to R, following the curve of the ring. Clip both HC ends to 3 inches and glue to wrong side.
4. Repeat step 3.
5. Divide WC into 6 equal groups and knot 4½ SK in groups 1 and 6; 2½ SK in groups 2 and 5; and 1 SK in groups 3 and 4.
6. Using one ¾-yard length of red as HC, knot 2 rows of DHH, 1 from L to R and 1 from R to L.
7. Knot 8 AHH with cords 1 and 2, then with cords 23 and 24; knot 3 AHH with cords 3 and 4, then with cords 21 and 22; knot 2 AHH with cords 5 and 6, then with cords 19 and 20. (Number WC from L to R.)
8. Divide orange WC into 3 equal groups; tie 3 decreasing rows of ASK, **(fig. 1)**.
9. Using the red WC as HC, knot 6 diagonal rows of DHH from UL and from UR to LC, dividing the orange WC into 2 equal groups and using them as DHH WC **(fig. 2)**. Divide the red WC into 6 pairs and knot 3 AHH with each pair. Add extra knots if needed to even out lengths.
10. Knot 14 AHH with orange cords 1 and 2, 23 and 24; knot 9 AHH with orange cords 3 and 4, 21 and 22.
11. Cross the 2 C red cords and knot 1 diagonal row of DHH from UC to LL and to LR, using the remaining red cords as WC.
12. Make a Berry Pattern, using 5 red WC at L as HC and 5 red WC at R as WC

(see page 20). Follow with 1 diagonal row of DHH from UL and from UR to LC.
13. Using the orange cords to the R and to the L of the Berry Pattern, tie 8 rows of DHH on each side as shown in **figure 3**. Divide the red WC into 6 pairs and knot 3 AHH in each pair.
14. Repeat steps 10, 9 (1st sentence only, but work from UC to LL and LR), 8 (knot 3 *increasing* rows of ASK), 7.
15. Repeat step 6 through 14.
16. Divide the red WC on L and R into 6 pairs and knot as follows: cords 1 and 2, 23 and 24—8 AHH; cords 3 and 4, 21 and 22—5 AHH; cords 5 and 6, 19 and 20—6 AHH. Knot 3 diagonal rows of DHH from ULC to LL at L and from URC to LR at R.
17. Repeat step 8.
18. Knot 3 diagonal rows of DHH from UL and from UR to LC, using only orange cords.
19. Divide all WC into 8 equal groups. Knot each red group into a 9-inch-long HK sinnet. Then join each pair of red sinnets with 2 SK **(fig. 4)**. Redivide the red WC back into 4 equal groups and add 9½ inches of HK to each sinnet.
20. Knot each group of orange WC into a 20-inch-long HK sinnet.
21. DHH all 4 orange sinnets to the back of the remaining ring and all 4 red sinnets to the front of the ring. OK all WC below the ring.
22. RMK the 14 doubled 1½-yard lengths of orange cord as follows: 4 RMK between red sinnets 1 and 2 and between red sinnets 3 and 4; 3 RMK to the L and to the R of the orange sinnets.
23. Repeat step 8 at the front of the ring, using C red cords and 1 pair of orange cords at either side as WC.
24. Repeat step 9, knotting only 3 diagonal rows of DHH; use orange cords as HC.
25. Repeat steps 23 and 24 at the back of the ring, using only orange WC and HC.
26. Using the 3½-yard length of red, wrap all ends together directly below the bottom DHH rows. Wrap for 2 inches, following the method given in step 2 on page 23. Cut all ends 14 inches from wrapping.
27. Weave lengths of wire in behind each horizontal row of DHH in the plant hanger.
28. Glue down all loose cord ends.

This red jute plant hanger deserves star billing in your home as well as on our cover. A stately column of knots ripples downward from a covered ring into a cuplike pot holder garnished with long fringe.

1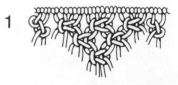

2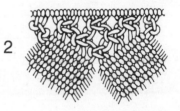

3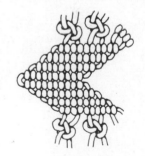

4

Cavandoli Clutch Purse

(Color photo on page 63)

Cavandoli knotting originated in Italy, where it was first taught to schoolchildren. This technique employs only two knots to create a two-color design. Our folk art clutch purse is decorated with two simple designs, both of which can be worked from the pattern graphs on the facing page. Each empty square on the graph equals one double half hitch knot; each filled square indicates one vertical double half hitch knot.

Materials: Thirty-nine 2½-yard lengths, nine 1-yard lengths, and two 20-inch lengths of black 3-ply wool rug yarn; one 30-yard length, one 4-yard length, and two ½-yard lengths of red 3-ply wool rug yarn; ¼ yard of heavy black lining material; 7-inch black zipper; blunt tapestry needle; regular sewing needle; black sewing thread.

How to make:

1. The body of this purse is begun at its center, which will later form the bottom of the finished purse. Pin the midpoint of the 30-yard length of red cord (hereafter referred to as "pattern cord," or "PC") to the working surface and mount twenty 2½-yard black WC at their midpoints to the L of the pin with DHH **(fig. 1)**; then mount the remaining 2½-yard lengths to the R of the pin with DHH. Pin the R PC end aside, for you will be working with the L PC.

2. Starting from the L, work row 2 in this order: 3 DHH † 3 VDHH, 3 DHH *. Repeat starred sequence 6 more times to complete the row.

3. Knot a row of DHH from R to L.

4. For the next 19 rows, follow the graph for the main design pattern, *working from the bottom up.* The design will appear in an upside-down position.

5. Knot a row of DHH from R to L.

6. Knot a row of VDHH from L to R, working over 2 HC at a time. The last knot in the row has only 1 HC, for a total of 20 VDHH.

7. Knot a row of DHH from R to L.

8. For the final row, knot a series of individual LH over the PC **(fig. 2)** and cut all cord ends (including the PC) to 1½ inches, folding them to the wrong side of the purse.

9. For the 2nd half of the purse, turn the piece upside-down and again work out from the center of the purse. Repeat steps 2 through 8, reading L instead of R and R instead of L.

10. Begin one side panel in the fol-

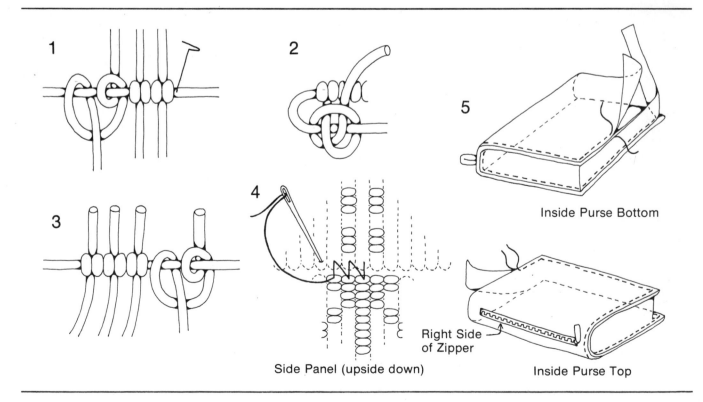

Side Panel (upside down)

Inside Purse Bottom

Right Side of Zipper

Inside Purse Top

lowing manner: At the R end of the 4-yard PC, tie an OK and pin it to the working surface.

11. Mount the nine 1-yard WC to the PC from R to L, using RMK and leaving 1½-inch ends above the PC **(fig. 3)**.

12. Work downward from the top of the secondary design (20 rows). When the panel is completed, trim all ends (including the PC) to 1½ inches.

13. Repeat step 12 for other side panel.

14. To construct the purse, thread a 20-inch length of black yarn onto the tapestry needle; then start at the corner of one end of the purse body and attach it to the centermost row (the stem of the flower) of 1 side panel as shown in **figure 4**. As you work, shape the bottom, sides, and top of the purse body around the side panel so that both ends meet evenly at the purse top.

15. Repeat for the other side panel.

16. To line the purse, cut the following from the lining fabric: two 2½ by 4½-inch rectangles; two 5 by 7-inch rectangles; and one 2½ by 7-inch rectangle.

17. Attach the 7-inch zipper to the 2 large lining pieces along the longest sides, following package directions.

18. Using a ½-inch seam allowance, sew the two 4½-inch-long rectangles to either end of the 2½ by 6-inch rectangle to make one continuous strip. To form the boxlike lining, attach this strip to the wrong side of the zippered lining pieces as in **figure 5**, starting on one short end and ending at the other. This means that the zipper tongue will be on the same side as the seam allowances.

19. To make purse loop, knot a 6-inch chain of AHH. Double the chain and knot the 4 strands together firmly; then pass 2 ends under and 2 ends over the PC of one of the side panels to meet on the inside of the purse. Knot with 2 SK to attach the loop firmly to the purse.

20. *Do not* turn the lining but drop it into the purse, fitting it into place as snugly as possible with raw edges facing the wrong side of the macramé.

21. Hand-stitch the lining to the open lip of the purse with black thread.

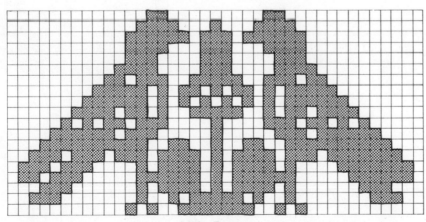

Main Pattern

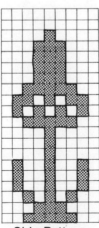

Side Pattern

Lacy Choker Necklace

(Color photo on page 63)

Demurely delicate, this lacy choker band is an ideal project for a beginner. The band is based on a simple repeat pattern using only one knot, the double half hitch.

Materials: Two 5/16-inch-diameter glass beads; eight 2½-yard strands of black #18 waxed nylon cord; white glue.

How to make:

1. Find the midpoint of each cord; then, holding all cords together, knot them as 1 into an OK 1 inch from their midpoints **(fig. 1)**. Pin OK to working surface.

2. Pass 1 bead onto the 2 centermost WC, leaving 3 WC on each side of the bead.

3. Using the outside cords on either edge as WC, tie a series of 6 RMK over each of the remaining pairs of cords as shown in **figure 2**, spacing knots 2, 3, 4, and 5 each ¼ inch apart. Push head up tight against OK; then push all RMK's up against each other to surround bead with tight knots and loops.

4. Leaving the outermost cord on each edge free, divide the remaining 6 cords into 3 pairs and tie a SK over the C pair, using each of the remaining 2 pairs as though they were 1 cord **(fig. 3)**.

5. Divide the cords into 2 groups of 4 cords each; then work diagonally out from UC to LL and LR, tying 3 diminishing rows of DHH on each side **(fig. 4)**.

6. Repeat step 5 from UC to LL and LR, crossing the 2 centermost cords and using them as the 1st HC.

7. Repeat steps 4 through 6 eight times.

8. Again repeat steps 4 through 6; then use the far L and far R cord on each edge to tie 2 pairs of diagonal rows of DHH from UL and UR to LC. Knot off each WC end tightly against the last DHH row. Clip off WC ends and dip knots in white glue.

9. For 2nd half of necklace, remove the OK at choker midpoint; then repeat steps 4 through 6 ten times.

10. Repeat step 5; then OK, clip off, and glue each of the 3 outside WC on each edge, leaving the 2 WC at C uncut.

11. Slip the clasp bead onto both remaining cords; then bring each cord end up, over, and around itself above the bead. At this point, tie a firm SK **(fig. 5)**, clip the 2 cord ends, and coat the SK with white glue to secure it.

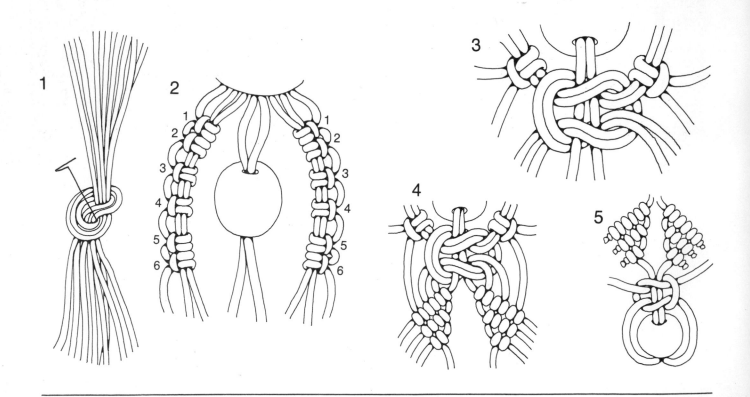

A

B. Lacy Choker Necklace, page 62

A delicate Victorian period piece, this tiny lacelike choker harkens back to the days of throat ribbons and cameos. Fine waxed nylon cord determines its diminutive scale. Design: Luisita Amiguet.

B

A. Cavandoli Clutch Purse, page 60

An Italian macramé technique reproduces charming folk art patterns on the sides of this red and deep gray woolen clutch purse. Only two knots are used to create a two-color effect. Design: Hannalies Penner.

Sampler Shoulder Bag

(Color photo on page 66)

This unusual purse will give you a chance to use some interesting repeat patterns, macramé and otherwise. Latticework, modified diamonds with gathering knots, alternating bobble knots, and even simple weaving come together in the texturally rich overall appearance of this advanced project.

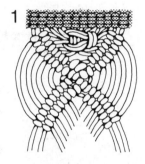

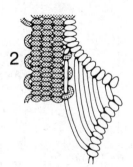

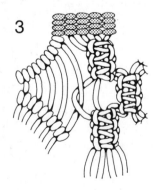

Materials: One 10-inch length, twenty-four 6-yard lengths, two 5-yard lengths, and eight 2-yard lengths of 3-ply purple rug yarn; two 15-yard lengths, two 2-yard lengths, two 5-yard lengths, two 1½-yard lengths, and one ½-yard length of 3-ply gray rug yarn; 2½ yards each of gray, orange, and yellow 3-ply rug yarn; ½ yard of ocher yellow cotton lining fabric; yellow thread; needle.

How to make:

1. OK each end of the 10-inch length of purple cord (to be used as HC) and pin both knots to the working surface.

2. Mount cord lengths in this order (from L to R): one 15-yard length of gray folded to make one 14-yard WC and one 1-yard WC (the 14-yard WC should be on the L edge), one 2-yard gray length at its midpoint, twenty-four 6-yard purple lengths at their midpoints, one 2-yard gray length at its midpoint, and one 15-yard length folded to make one 1-yard WC and one 14-yard WC (the 14-yard WC should be on the R edge).

3. Using the R 14-yard cord as WC, knot 2 rows of VDHH, 1 from R to L and 1 from L to R.

4. Divide the purple WC into the following 3 groups (L to R): 12, 24, 12.

5. To begin the column of modified diamonds using the L group of 12 WC, hold the C 4 WC in a bundle and tie 1 SK over them, using each pair of cords directly to the R and to the L as 1 WC. Using the 2 remaining outside WC on both sides as HC, knot 2 curving diagonal rows of DHH in from UL and UR, joining all 4 rows at LC.

6. Following this join, continue to use the outside WC pairs as HC by crossing them and knotting 2 more curving rows of DHH outward from UC to LL and LR **(fig. 1)**.

7. Repeat steps 5 and 6 on the R side.

8. Repeat steps 5 and 6 three times on the L side and 8 times on the R side.

9. At this point, use the long gray cords at either side of the piece as WC to knot 52 rows of VDHH down each edge of the purse, interlocking every other inner loop with the far L and far R WC of the 2 modified diamond columns **(fig. 2)**. Finish with the WC at the outside edges; then set all gray cords aside.

10. For the alternating bobble pattern (see page 20) at the middle, divide the 24 C purple WC into 6 groups of 4 WC each and knot 6 bobbles, 1 in each group.

11. Redivide the 24 WC into 5 groups of 4 WC each, linking the 2 unused outer WC at each side with the outside loops of the adjacent modified diamond patterns **(fig. 3)**, and knot a second row of 5 bobbles.

12. Repeat step 10.

From this point on, for stability, interlock every other loop of any pattern with the nearest loop or cord of its adjacent pattern throughout the purse.

13. Use the outside purple WC from the last far R bobble as a HC for 2 rows of DHH, from R to L and from L to R below the bobble pattern area only. Interlock the HC at the L after the first DHH row.

14. Mount one 2-yard length of purple to the outside purple WC from the far L bobble, as in **figure 4**. Use this cord as WC to knot twenty 2-knot rows of VDHH, using the 2 outermost cords on the L as HC and making 2 vertical columns. Leave slight loops at the inside of the 2 columns and interlock every other outside loop of the WC through the nearest cord of the adjacent modified diamond pattern. When the rows are completed, eliminate the added WC.

15. Repeat step 14 on the R side, mounting the 2-yard length of purple on the far R bobble WC.

16. Following the color photograph on page 66 for color placement, weave lengths of orange, gray, and yellow into the purple WC at the center of the purse **(fig. 5)**. Leave 3 inches free at the beginning and at the end of each color length and cut off any excess colored cord, setting it aside for later use.

17. Use the far L purple HC from the VDHH columns as HC for 2 rows of DHH below the woven area, 1 from L to R and 1 from R to L.

18. Repeat steps 10 through 12 for lower bobble area.

19. Using the outside cord in the far R bobble knot as HC, knot 2 rows of DHH, 1 from R to L and 1 from L to R. These rows should run below the bobble and the left modified diamond sections to and from the gray area along the L edge.

20. Repeat step 9, knotting these columns as you work. The easiest way is to knot them in 3 steps, working them simultaneously with the central design areas.

21. As in **figure 4**, mount one 2-yard length of purple to the 15th purple cord in from the L. Use this cord as WC and cords 1 and 2 as HC to knot 3 inches of VDHH in 2 columns. Leave loops along the R side of the column and link the L loops of the column to the adjacent gray column.

22. Mount one 2-yard length of purple to the far L purple WC; use this cord as WC and cords 1 and 2 as HC to knot 3 inches of VDHH In 2 columns. Leave loops along each side of the column.

23. Following the color photograph on page 66, weave strands of orange, yellow, and gray through the area between both vertical columns of VDHH, interlocking them with the loops of the columns at either side.

24. Divide the purple cords falling between the modified diamond column and the VDHH column to the R of the woven area into 5 equal groups of 4 WC each. As in **figure 6**, use the far R WC of each group as HC and knot 5 diagonal segments of 3 DHH each from UR to LL.

25. Use the 2nd WC in each group as HC and knot 4 diagonal segments of 3 DHH each from UL to LR, knotting a partial row at the far R **(fig. 7)**.

26. Repeat steps 24 and 25 four more times to complete this section.

27. Repeat step 24.

28. Use the far L purple WC as HC to tie a row of DHH from the gray area at L to the column of modified diamonds at R.

29. Repeat step 28, working from R to L and ending at the gray area.

30. Repeat steps 21 through 29, but reverse the woven and the latticework areas. The VDHH columns in step 20 should fall on the R edge, the woven area

should cover 16 purple cords, and the VDHH columns in step 21 should fall immediately to the L of the woven area. For the 2nd latticework area, work as follows: divide the 16 purple WC on the L into 4 equal groups and repeat steps 24 and 25 six times to complete the section.

31. Repeat steps 21 through 29, but knot 2-inch-long VDHH columns and repeat steps 23 and 24 four times.

32. Using the far L WC as HC, knot 1 row of DHH from L to R, incorporating all WC.

33. Knot 2 rows of VDHH, using the far L gray cord as WC and working 1st from L to R, then from R to L.

34. Using the outside L and the outside R cords as WC, knot 1 final row of VDHH in each gray column.

35. Using the far L purple WC as HC, knot 1 final row of DHH from L to R; end the DHH row when the last purple WC is used.

36. Clip all cord ends to 2 inches and iron them toward the wrong side of the purse.

37. To line the purse, cut the lining 2 inches larger all around than the purse body. Iron under a 1-inch seam allowance on all sides of the lining; then slipstitch the lining to the wrong side of the macramé, keeping the lining slightly back from the loops along each edge.

38. To join the sides of the purse, fold It in half, wrong sides together, and use 1½-yard lengths of gray cord to lace the loops together as in **figure 8**. Knot off the ends at the inside of the purse on each joined edge.

39. Form the handle of the purse as follows: mount two 5-yard lengths of purple and of gray at their midpoints to 1 corner of the purse, making 4 purple WC and 4 gray WC. Knot 2 separate 16-inch-long HK sinnets, 1 in each color; when the sinnets are completed, twist them around each other to form a 2-color handle. OK each WC and thread ends out through the opposite corner of the purse. Use a ½-yard length of gray cord to group the cord ends into a tassel, wrapping for 1½ inches directly below the top edge of the purse. Trim the tassel to measure 6 inches.

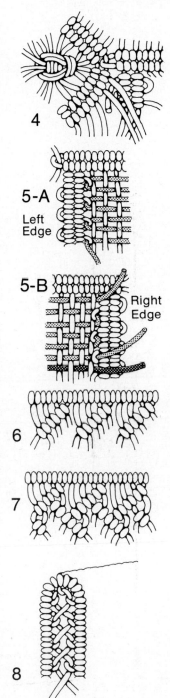

4

5-A
Left Edge

5-B
Right Edge

6

7

8

A. Reverse of the purse: *Simple weaving is mixed with interwoven macramé bars on the back of this intricate bag, pictured here to make its construction an easier task.*

B. Sampler Shoulder Bag, page 64

Bobbles, braids, and interwoven segments combine in an intriguing series of surface treatments on this small but striking shoulder bag. Resembling a macramé sampler when knotted together, the patterns are nevertheless arranged in a predetermined manner. Design: Gerta Wingerd.

B

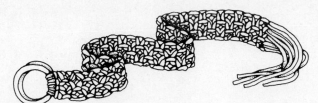

Leather Thong Belt

Materials: Four 7-yard lengths of square-cut, 3/16-inch-wide leather thong; two 2-inch-diameter brass belt rings.

How to make:

1. Fold each 7-yard length of thong in half; then attach each doubled length at the fold to both rings at once **(fig. 1)**. This will give you 8 WC. Bobbin each WC and secure with a rubber band; then anchor the rings to your working surface.

2. Divide the WC into 2 groups of 4 cords each and tie 2 SK as shown in **figure 2**.

3. Using the center 4 lengths and, leaving the outer pairs free, tie 1 SK **(fig. 3)**.

4. Repeat steps 2 and 3 until the belt is long enough to go around the waist and through the loop with about 3 inches extra. Cut cord ends as desired for fringe.

This belt has some good things going for it: expandable design, simple construction, and the use of a durable material—leather thong. Made completely with alternating square knots, this is a good project for the beginner. If you can't locate leather thong, cut your own from a single large piece of ⅛-inch-thick leather. Draw a circle on it and, starting at the outside edge work spirally to the center, cutting a continuous, 3/16-inch-wide thong with a sharp knife or heavy-duty scissors.

No knotty problems here; just a simple alternate square knot pattern to give you a rugged belt of leather thong. Design: The Leatherworks.

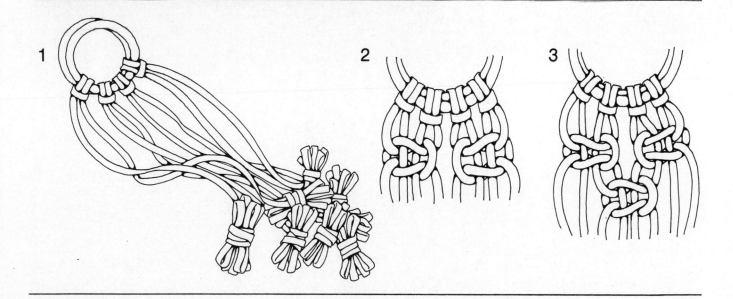

Sea and Sand Necklace

(Color photo on page 70)

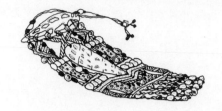

Shades of the beach—they're all here in this pleasingly precise necklace. A true tour de force for the advanced knotter, this piece depends on planning and careful workmanship for a professional look.

Materials: Twenty 3-yard lengths, sixteen 1½-yard lengths, and three 1-yard lengths of taupe #18 waxed nylon cord; two 2-yard lengths and three 1-yard lengths of warm ivory #18 waxed nylon cord; one cross-section and one slab-cut side of a mitra or other shell; 23 orange Wili Wili seed beads (referred to as orange); 48 cylindrical shell beads (referred to as black); 28 round mother-of-pearl beads (referred to as white); white glue.

How to make:

1. For one *neck cord,* fold two 3-yard lengths of taupe cord in half and mount individually to L edge of shell cross-section.

2. Begin the cord in this manner: 1 SK; 2 black beads, 1 on each outside cord; 1 SK; 1 orange bead over both center cords together; 1 SK; 2 black beads, 1 on each outside cord.

3. Tie 8 inches of AHH chain, using pairs of cords as single cord units (see Half Hitch Chains, step 2, page 15).

4. Tie an OK with all 4 cords; then thread a black bead onto each cord end and secure each bead with an OK. Dip each knot in white glue to secure it.

5. Repeat steps 1 through 4 for 2nd neck cord, working at R edge.

6. To begin pendant portion of necklace, divide sixteen 3-yard lengths of taupe cord into 4 groups of 3 cords each and 2 groups of 2 cords each. Using each group as though it were a single unit, fold in half and mount at fold to R and L sides of shell cross-section, working from *outside* in. L side: 3-cord group, 3-cord group, 2-cord group. R side: 3-cord group, 3-cord group, 2-cord group, leaving 1¼ inches of shell free at the LC edge.

From this point on, only the left-hand side of the pendant will be explained; for the right side, work simultaneously, reversing all directions to read R instead of L and L instead of R.

7. Number L cords from outside in (1 to 16); cords for the C shell pendant are explained in step 43. Hold cord 12 diagonally to LL, then lay in 1 end of a 2-yard length of ivory cord. Using both cords as 1 HC,

tie a diagonal row of DHH from R to L (**fig. 1**), adding an orange bead to cord 3 before knotting it on. Trim off short end of ivory cord.

8. With the ivory cord, tie a diagonal row of VDHH from UR to LL, leaving the last cord free; follow it with a diagonal row of DHH, using UR taupe cord as HC. Leave the 2 outside cords free.

9. Using cord 9 as HC, tie a SK with cords 8 and 10; add a black bead; tie a SK; add another black bead; tie a last SK.

10. Tie 6 diagonal decreasing rows of DHH from UR to LL, leaving cords 12, ivory, and 11 free (**fig. 2**).

11. Working diagonally from UL to LR, use cord 11 as HC and tie a row of DHH followed by a row of VDHH ending in a DHH. Finish with a diagonal row of DHH, using cord 12 as HC (**fig. 3**).

12. Work cords 13 to 16 as shown in **figure 4**, using a 1-yard length of ivory cord at its midpoint as the initial HC for row 1. Join right and left sides of this part of the design by tying a SK with the ivory cords (**fig. 5**).

13. Using both L ivory cords coming from the SK as one HC, tie 4 horizontal decreasing rows of DHH from R to L; then tie 4 vertical decreasing rows of DHH from top to bottom, moving to L (**fig. 6**).

14. Repeat step 13; then cut away 1 of the 2 ivory HC. Join the 2nd completed section to the 1st completed section. To do this, use the far L taupe cord of the 2nd section to tie 1 DHH over the ivory HC from the 1st section and 1 DHH at the end of the last diagonal row of knots in the 1st section.

15. Thread 1 orange bead onto the far L taupe cord.

16. Using the far R ivory cord as a HC, work a row of DHH horizontally from R to L. After tying 3 knots in the row, include the second ivory HC, using it as one with the taupe HC. After tying 5 more knots cut away the 2nd ivory HC.

17. Tie a horizontal row of VDHH from L to R with the ivory cord.

18. Repeat 1st sentence of step 16.

19. Thread 1 white bead onto each of the following cords: far L ivory cord, taupe cords 5, 11, and 16.

20. Repeat 1st sentence of step 16.

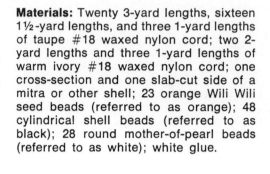
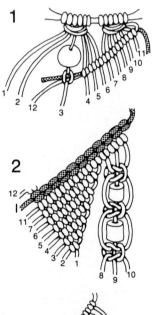

21. Repeat step 17.

22. Repeat step 18.

23. At *each side* of the section being worked, use 4 cords to knot a chain of beads and SK as follows: 1 SK; 1 black bead on 2 C cords; 1 SK; 1 orange bead on 1 C cord; 1 SK; 1 black bead on 2 C cords; 1 SK. Conceal the ivory cord on the R side by running it down through the centers of the knots and beads in the R chain.

24. With the remaining 8 cords, tie 10 rows of ASK.

25. Repeat 1st sentence of step 16.

26. Repeat steps 17 through 19.

27. Repeat 1st sentence of step 16; then with HC held diagonally down from L to R, add eight 1½-yard lengths of folded taupe cord at their midpoints. Use the picot mount described on page 22, step 1. At the center of the necklace, cross holding cords as in **figure 7**.

28. Using all cords, repeat step 17, but work upward diagonally and then horizontally from LRC to UL edge.

29. Repeat step 16, working from R to L and using cord 16 as HC.

30. Repeat 3 times the section shown in **figure 8**, using taupe cord 1 as the continuous zigzag HC and incorporating the ivory HC from the diagonal row of VDHH only when moving from UR to LL. At end of the 3rd repeat, cut away the ivory cord.

31. Tie 7 rows of ASK with the remaining 12 cords.

32. Working on the central portion, use the 1st added cord on the L edge to tie a diagonal row of DHH from UL to LRC. Follow with 2 more rows, using 2nd and 3rd cords respectively as HC. Join *only the last row* to its mate at C of the necklace **(fig. 9)**.

33. Using cord 4 as HC, tie a diagonal row of VDHH from UL to LRC; join it to its mate at C **(fig. 9)**.

34. Knot a final diagonal row of DHH from UL to LRC, using cord 5 as HC. Join it to its mate at center of the necklace **(fig. 9)**.

35. Divide cords on L side of C into 4 groups of 4 cords each. Tie 1 SK with each group of 4 cords; add 1 black bead to C 2 cords of each group and secure each with a SK. Tie an OK with the 2 C cords

and thread on an orange bead, securing it with an OK.

36. Beginning from the L edge of the ASK area worked in step 24, continue to knot rows of ASK, gradually incorporating all remaining cords on the R except the 2 WC through the orange bead. After the last group of 4 cords is tied in, work 5 more rows of ASK. Incorporate the 2 C cords and join both sides of the necklace in the 5th row **(fig. 10)**.

37. To join all sections at the bottom, add in a 2-yard length of ivory cord, starting it 6 inches to the L of the lower edge of the necklace. Hold the longer end horizontally and tie a row of DHH from L to R with all WC.

38. Follow with a horizontal row of VDHH from R to L.

39. Repeat last sentence of step 37.

40. Repeat step 39, working from R to L.

41. Divide L half of cords into the following groups, working from L to C: 5, 6, 5, 5, 6, 5. On each group use the 2 outside cords as WC and the rest as HC for a sinnet of HK. Include ivory cord in the core of the far L sinnet to conceal.

42. Tie each sinnet as follows: 25 HK; add 1 black bead; 5 HK, add 1 white bead; 8 HK, add 1 orange bead; secure with OK; trim excess cord; dip knot in glue.

43. To add inner shell pendant: attach 3 folded 1-yard lengths of taupe cord as 1 group to the very center of the shell cross-section with a MK.

44. Using 2 center cords as HC, tie 2 matching diagonal rows of DHH from UC to LL and LR.

45. Center a 1-yard length of ivory cord under the rows in step 44; then use it to tie 2 matching diagonal rows of VDHH from UC to LL and LR.

46. Repeat step 44.

47. Using outside taupe cords as HC, knot 2 diagonal rows of DHH from UL and UR to LC, using all cords.

48. Pass all but the 2 HC through the *front* of the shell pendant and adjust placement of shell to necklace. Pull ends upward *behind* shell cross section and knot 4 SK with remaining 2 HC over all cords holding the shell. Cut off and glue the WC to secure. Cut off all HC as close as possible to the top SK.

5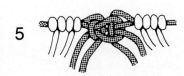

6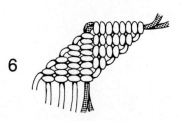

7

8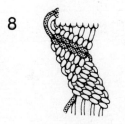

9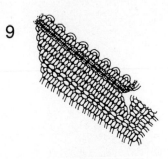

10
Center Cords

**Sea and Sand Necklace,
page 68**

Framed in waxed nylon knotting, sliced mitra shells echo in the burnt orange and black bead accents dotted throughout this elegant piece of beach-colored body jewelry.
Design: Edwina Hawbecker.

A. Snappy Strap Bracelet, page 73

Variety is the spice of life. And variety's what you get when this monotone waxed nylon strap bracelet is enlivened with the addition of cords in one, two, or three extra colors.
Design: Barbara Jee.

B. Oriental Belt, page 72

Overlapping diamond and sphere elements form a filigreelike belt length of golden nylon twine. Based on a repeat pattern, this belt is well within the scope of the beginner.
Design: Barbara Jee.

B

Oriental Belt

(Color photo on page 71)

Add style to your slacks with this openwork belt of nylon twine. A simple repeat pattern easy enough for a beginner to tackle forms the main design of the belt. For waist measurements over 28 inches (the belt size presented here), add 8 inches per cord for each additional inch needed.

Materials: Eight 10-yard lengths of gold nylon twine; one belt buckle with a 1¼-inch-wide buckle bar; needle with large eye; white glue.

How to make:

1. Hold the buckle with its back side *toward* you, making sure that its tongue in its correct position hangs downward. Mount the midpoint of each cord onto the buckle bar with MK. This gives 16 WC.

2. Use the 2 centermost cords as HC for diagonal rows of DHH worked from UC to LL and LR. Repeat twice for 3 consecutive rows **(fig. 1)**.

3. Using the 2 outside cords on either edge, tie 2 chains of 6 AHH **(fig. 2)**.

4. Use the remaining 12 cords to make a diamond-shaped area of 5 rows of ASK, starting ¼ inch below the last design area (see **figure 3**, below, right).

5. Using all 16 cords, leave another ¼-inch space and tie 3 consecutive diagonal rows of DHH from UL and UR edges to LC **(fig. 4)**.

6. With the 2 outermost groups of 3 cords each from either side, tie chains of 12 LH and 8 LH **(fig. 5)**.

7. Tie a chain of 4 SK at C, with 2 cords as WC and the 2 C cords as HC.

8. Repeat steps 2 through 7 nine times, ending with the pattern given in step 2.

9. Starting with the center 4 cords and gradually increasing outward until all cords are in use, tie 38 rows of ASK. Tie 3 more rows of ASK decreasing to 3, then 2, and ending with 1 central SK **(fig. 6)**.

10. Repeat step 5, but tie only 2 rows.

11. Press cords to the back of the belt and sew them down with matching thread. Trim off excess cord and glue into place.

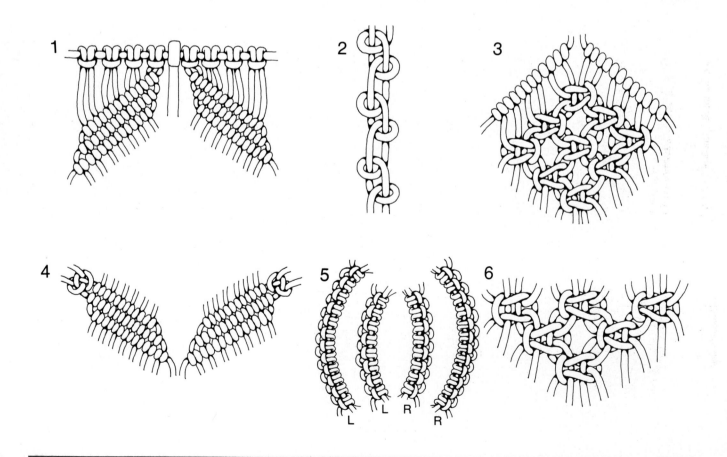

Snappy Strap Bracelet

(Color photo on page 71)

Materials: 20 yards of buff-colored #18 waxed nylon cord cut into eight 2½-yard strands (for the other straps shown, use 2½-yard strands of each color desired in the following orders: 3 black, 2 ivory, 3 black; 1 green, 1 orange, 2 yellow, 1 orange, 1 green; or 1 green, 1 light green, 1 blue, 2 white, 1 blue, 1 light green, 1 green); ⅝-inch brass buckle; 2 small ¼-inch-diameter beads; needle with large eye; white glue.

How to make:

1. Hold the buckle with its back side *toward* you, making sure that its tongue in its correct position hangs downward. Mount each cord at its midpoint onto the buckle bar, 4 cords to a side (giving 16 WC).

2. Tie 16 rows of ASK, starting row 1 with 4 SK and ending row 16 with 3 SK. This will leave both outside cord pairs in row 16 hanging free and untied.

3. For rows 17 and 18, knot as indicated in **figure 1**, coming to a point at C.

4. Using the outside cords as HC, tie diagonal rows of DHH, crossing them at C **(fig. 2)**.

5. Repeat step 4.

6. Using the outside cords as WC, tie diagonal rows of VDHH, crossing at C **(fig. 3)**.

7. Repeat step 4 twice.

8. Thread a bead onto the 2 C cords.

9. Tie 2 matching SK chains of 5 knots each with the 3 cords at either side of the bead **(fig. 4)**.

10. With the 4 outside cords at each edge, tie 2 matching SK chains of 8 knots each.

11. Using the 2 C cords as HC, tie diagonal rows of DHH from UC to LL and LR edges **(fig. 5)**.

12. Repeat step 11, crossing HC.

13. Tie 19 ASK rows from this point on, beginning with the 4 C cords and gradually increasing to the use of all 16 cords.

14. For the 2nd half of the strap, repeat the preceding steps in the following order: 3 (change to read " . . . rows 20 and 21 . . ."), 4, 8, 9, 10, 11, 12, 6 (use the 2 C cords as WC), 11, 12, 13 (knot 27 rows), 3 (change to read " . . . rows 28 and 29 . . ."), 4, and 5.

15. Turn the strap on its face and press the WC flat against the back. Holding down the cords, sew them to the back side with a thread pulled from an unraveled length of nylon cord. Cut off loose ends and secure them with white glue.

Designed for the talents of an intermediate macramé buff, this wrist strap depends on firm, regular knotting for its good looks. If you're feeling adventurous, try expanding it into a choker or a belt.

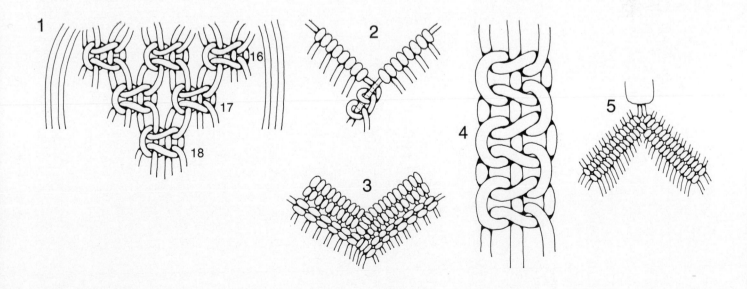

For capitalized abbreviations, see Knotting Key on page 35.

Macramé Masterworks

In a very short time span, macramé has progressed from revived craft to sophisticated art form. To inspire and intrigue you, we present here a selection of current works by some of the finest artists in this field.

A. "Berries and Beads" necklace employs golden picots, Berry knots, and chains intermixed with jade-blue beads. Design: Elaine Seely.

B. Josephine knot necklace of waxed linen displays old Chinese coins. Plaited-in red cord runs through several knots. Design: Nilda Duffek.

A   B

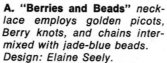

C

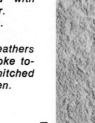

C. Exploding colors arc outward from the center of this spontaneously worked pendant. Design: Helen Bitar.

D. Earthy, found-object-laden necklace is macraméd with waxed linen and leather. Design: Joyce L. Barnes.

E. Sweep of hackle feathers frames 76 carats of smoke topaz quartz double half hitched together with waxed linen. Design: Paul Johnson.

D   E

A. Lion-faced mask *was looped, knotted, and woven of rope and cord into an exciting, three-dimensional shape. The techniques used to make the mask are based on those practiced by the primitive native artists of New Guinea. Design: Rubin Steinberg.*

B

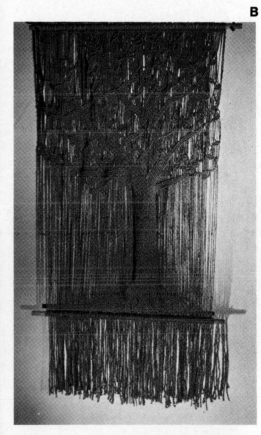

B. Tree hanging *is a floating Cavandoli work in brown jute knotted with double half hitches from a pattern taped to the mounting dowel. Design: Susan Peters.*

C. "Persian Collar" *could be an ancient artifact; instead, it's a modern piece worked in Cavandoli knotting with fine copen blue and gold cords. Old carnelian points, beads, and brass filigree lend a feeling of antiquity. Design: Sylvia Cook.*

C

A

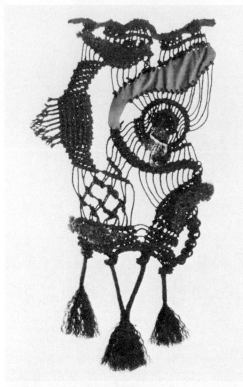

B

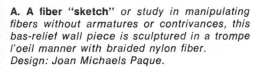

A. A fiber "sketch" or study in manipulating fibers without armatures or contrivances, this bas-relief wall piece is sculptured in a trompe l'oeil manner with braided nylon fiber.
Design: Joan Michaels Paque.

B. "Nesting Place" resembles an ancient clothing fragment. Sisal, suede, carpet shag, and feathers are combined in this unusual exploration of negative and positive space.
Design: Nancy Robb Dunst.

C. "Intellectual-in-the-Clouds," a potpourri of macramé, weaving, assemblage, and porcelain ceramic work, was constructed over a welded steel form. Mink tails appear in the tassels.
Design: Edwina Drobny.

D. "Perchance to Dream" is the culmination of a number of techniques. Macramé and wrapping were used to construct the halo of hair and the dramatic wings of this angel.
Design: Nancy and Dewey Lipe.

C

D

B

A. Arched doorway curtain of white cotton cording was knotted entirely of square knots and double half hitches in matching panels. Design: Peggy Stone.

B. Baby's "bed" is completely handcrafted, down to the butternut wood frame. Soft cotton welting is knotted across the frame, anchored, and then wrapped in areas with colored jute. Design: Susan Peters.

C. Refined design elevates to the realm of art this practical window planter of upholsterer's cord. Several wooden hoops knotted into the design support the plant saucers. Design: Esther Parada.

D. Clock face adds an element of surprise to this tarred marlin plant hanger. Knotting was worked around wooden plaque-mounted clock. Design: Donalie Orton.

C

D

A. "Pocahontas Dress" could have been worn by the lady herself. It's a totem of Indian ancestry with feathers, shells, deer horn, leather, and tiny bells joined by natural fibers. Design: Jack Dunstan.

B. Muted colors interlock in a soft vest of wool rug yarn. Peacock down and Peking glass beads adorn the 147 handwrapped yarn tassels. Design: Pat Henshaw.

A

B

C

C. Abstracted shapes form a cityscape on the face of this intricately knotted pillow. Chains, double half hitches, and Cavandoli work are intermingled for a rich, textural effect. Design: Gerta Wingerd.

D

D. Multicolored belt is a white and bright concoction of shoelace cotton braid, double half hitched in separate rows and then wrapped with odds and ends of colored synthetic yarns. Design: Penny Laing.

A

B

A. Three months in the making, this 11-foot-tall fiber sculpture holds over 300 pounds of wrapped and knotted jute. *Design: Libby Platus.*

B. Linear background of vertical rows of double half hitches and wrapped openwork areas makes a graphic foil for the colorful, three-dimensional shapes knotted and interwoven across its surface with colored yarns. *Design: Marion Ferri.*

C

D

D. "Macramé Relief Number Two" makes use of entire lengths of half knot sinnets carefully arranged in blended color groups. Softly curved and folded back over itself, this piece has subtle surface changes and undulations, giving a three-dimensional effect. *Design: Michi Ouchi.*

C. Color control is supremely exhibited in this impressive wall hanging. Note the tapestry-like vine and leaf motifs, serving as bridges between more solidly knotted areas. *Design: Helen Freeman.*

Index

Photographers

Richard Anderson: 33 right. **Edward Bigelow:** 33 left. **Charles Bray:** 27 left. **Estelle Carlson:** 33 center. **Grace Chinn:** 26 left. **Edwina Drobney:** 76 bottom left. **Nancy Robb Dunst:** 76 top right. **Marion Ferri:** 28 left, 31 bottom left, 79 top right. **Winkie Fordney:** 29 bottom right center. **Alyson Smith Gonsalves:** 9 all, 25 all, 26 right, 29 top right, 31 top left, 32 left and center. **Mona Helcermanas-Benge:** 55 left, 70, 74 top left, 77 top left and bottom right, 78 all, back cover right. **Paul Johnson:** 31 top right, 74 bottom right. **William J. Kearns:** 74 bottom left. **Susan S. Lampton:** 28 right. **Dewey Lipe:** 76 bottom right. **Ells Marugg:** 7 all. **Jack McDowell:** 27 right, 31 bottom right. **John Satre Murphy:** 74 left center. **Museum of Fine Arts, Boston:** 4. **Akira Ouchi:** 79 bottom right. **Henry Paul Paque:** 76 top left. **Esther Parada:** 29 bottom right, 77 bottom left and top right. **Jack Peters:** 75 right. **Norman A. Plate:** 34, 39 all, 42 all, 47 all, 50 all, 55 right, 58 all, 63 all, 66 all, 67, 71 all, 74 top right, 75 bottom left, 79 bottom left, back cover left and bottom. **William C. Sedlacek:** 29 bottom left center. **William J. Shelley:** 29 top left, 31 bottom left, 32 right. **Rubin Steinberg:** 75 top left. **E. R. Vorenkamp:** 29 bottom left.